I AM NOT A PROPHET, THEREFORE I KNOW

Dispelling the Myth
We have to be Special
to Hear the Inner Voice

MARK C. HUGHES

KARMA PUBLISHING
Wilsonville, Oregon

Copyright © 2009 by Mark C. Hughes
Printed and bound in The United States of America

Cover and book design:
    Heather Kibbey, Northwest Publishers Consortium, www.npcbooks.com
Photography:
    Loma Smith, Loma Smith Photography, www.lomasmith.com

ISBN: 978-0-578-02338-0

KARMA PUBLISHING
PO Box 3554
Wilsonville, Oregon 97070-3554
(503) 819-3642
www.KarmaInstitute.org

DEDICATION

To my mother and father for their unconditional love and support
and willingness to suspend their need to understand,
and to my two children for their tolerance and
sense of humor when fielding the question,
"What does your Dad do?"

Kelsey,

The wisdom of the heart
is not just from this lifetime but
from the ages of our previous
lives. Pull upon your wisdom
and trust you are taking the
right steps.

all The best,

Mark

ACKNOWLEDGMENTS

I am who I am, I am where I am today, because of the influence of many people and many lessons learned. To my loving family growing up at Hume Street; thank you Leroy Moore for believing in me, Bert Johnson for inspiring me; The Neptune Dolphins, the four-man go-cart made of retired tricycles, double bed bunkbeds; Carol Johanson for trying something different, Otto t'Hooft, and Barbara West for opening my eyes to Lifespring, Reiki, and The Findhorn Foundation; The Island of Mull, being stranded in Munich, Bill Hawkey and The Dome of the Rock; The Eugene Hilton and Symmington Limousine Service, Katherine Wilson, "Homer and Eddie", Paul Tucker, Bob Rolsky, "Bartles and Jaymes", Margie Lundell, and the security guard at Universal Studios; "Selis, Selis & Hughes", The Living Enrichment Center, Productive Learning & Leisure, my Hispanic friend at the Nikken meeting; Jody Stephenson, Susie Walton, Delayne Guardini, John Moses, Tully Alford, and Benson Medina for being a mirror in many ways; and (for the tougher lessons in life), Bruce, Brian, and Chris; Loma, for my first check, her loving support, and for the incredible pictures on this book; to Lori, for allowing me to be, and Heather, for holding my hand; and for the fabulous memories when we were all together, to Kimberly, Taylor, and Nicholas for the best years of my life; to my Inner Voice that didn't give up on me when I lost hope, lost faith, lost my way; and, lastly, to all my friends, family, and acquaintances that came my way. Thank you. I am "internally" grateful.

TABLE OF CONTENTS

Foreword 1

Introduction 4

"In Search of the Elusive Truth" 15
    Looking Inward vs. Out There

"Universal Energy and Allowing it to Flow" 27
    It's all the Same: Open Up to It

"Just Be Still" 33
    Be Quiet

"Listening Comes In Many Ways" 41
    Be Open to The Many Ways God Speaks to Us

"Getting it Right" 49
    There is No Right Way to Meditate

"No Picking and Choosing Allowed" 59
    Trust vs. Fear: We Don't Get to Choose

"Taking Baby Steps" 67
    Building Confidence and a Connection to the Inner Voice

"Faith and Courage" 77
    Blind Faith is Required to Activate the Inner Voice

"It's Easier to Not Listen" 85
    To Sustain the Inner Voice You must Be Courageous

"Don't Try to Understand" 95
    Accepting the Inner Voice without Questioning

"There are No Guarantees With Listening" 103
    The Inner Voice Does Not Always Guarantee Positive Outcomes

"Be Open to Detours" 109
    Be Open to Change and New Opportunities

"Let Go of Your Attachment to the Outcome"..............................119
   Letting Go of What You Expect to Come Your Way

"It's Not Like Riding a Bike: Routine is Essential" 127
   Routine isn't Important, It is Imperative

"God is Like an Answering Machine" 133
   If You Want the Guidance, You Have to Respond

"The Willingness to Be" 139
   Be vs. Do

"Look at Life From a Whole New Perspective" 149
   Everything is Perfect, Just Perfect

"It Can Go Both Directions" 159
   Having a dialogue with The Inner Voice

"I Don't Need to Be Special" 167
   Dispelling the Myth

Epilogue 175
   It's About Readjusting, Rebalancing

FOREWORD

It's been nearly twenty years since I was directed to write this book. However, I had convinced myself I was not qualified to write a book, let alone take on such a topic as this. After all, "who am I" to write a book on such a profound topic as the Inner Voice? Oh, I have an incredible library. I have every kind of self help book you can think of ranging from meditation to past life regressions to communications to co-dependency. But you know I haven't finished reading one of them. Can you relate to that? I wrote this book for those of us that want to read shorter chapters and have the opportunity to reflect on what we have read before we read further.

While I struggled with my qualifications, I was driven, nevertheless, to tell my story. It is relayed to you without the influence of other authors, top selling books, clichés of the month. What you will experience in this book is my Inner Voice, my Divine Intelligence, my Inner Knowledge, my Higher Power speaking to me and through me. That part I cannot deny. That part is genuinely real, genuinely me, genuinely authentic. I don't get hooked on my need to know or understand everything. I only report what comes to me and I don't have an attachment to what I call it or if it makes sense. If you are comfortable calling it God or Your Higher Power or Your Intuition, it does not matter; I refer to it as my Inner Voice.

It is extremely important that I share how common I am, how ordinary. That is what this book is about: Dispelling the myth we have to be special to hear the Inner Voice. Being unaware as I have been, I hope I am able to share concepts and

1

ideas that many of you can relate to and most of you can benefit from. We don't have to be psychics or spiritual teachers. We can be laymen. We can be ordinary. We can be slow at figuring it out.

At one point, I considered calling the book, "I'm Dumber than I Look". How slow, how ignorant, how blind do we have to be before we figure it out; tapping into the Inner Voice is as common and as simple as taking a breath of air.

The search for guidance and direction is not out there as so many of us have come to believe. The message of this book is very simple: Listen to Your Inner Voice. We look outside of ourselves with the books we read, the tapes we listen to, the inspired lecture series we attend. The authentic search, however, is within; it is not out there.

If I could share my words so that you could hear them without writing a book, I would do so. Unfortunately, I am contributing to your search out there instead of within. I have, therefore, designed the book to be in short chapters that stand on their own; I ask that you read one chapter at a time and take two, five, ten times as long to reflect upon what you have read. I suggest you read the introduction and reflect on similarities in your life and consider making the changes you need to make as I share my awakening with each chapter I write, each exercise I present.

I will cover what I consider are some important concepts and then, at the end of each chapter, give you an opportunity to "Practice Being". You may journal your thoughts on your own or use my *I Am Not a Prophet Workbook* to guide you with some questions and pages to journal your thoughts.

Be patient with yourself; it only took me twenty frustrating years to grasp these simple concepts. Journaling your thoughts is a way I can encourage you to seek the answers from within; after all, that is what I want for you. Don't listen to me; listen to yourself.

If I could get you to come experience your journey with me, I would. I give numerous workshops on the theme, "Listening to Our Inner Voice" and the concept of "Dispelling The Myth We Have to Be Special." I speak primarily at business organizations, churches, and to young adults at colleges and universities across the United States. I hope you will join me some day. However, if you cannot, I have written this book from the heart and in a manner and style you would experience if you were with me in person...a free flow of spirit...the same Inner Knowledge that speaks so clearly to each and every one of us.

Promise me this: You will spend twice as much time in silence as you do reading this book, attending one of my workshops, or studying any other self-help book, audio tape series, or other "outside" source. I want you to experience the simple brilliance that comes from within rather than the abundance of guidance that comes from without. The journey is not in the search but in the personal awakening.

INTRODUCTION
I Didn't Listen

It was somewhere around the year of 1999. I arose from my bed and quietly placed my hooded terry cloth robe over my body and slipped down the hall to the living room. It was early morning. No one else was up. It was quiet and I could see the reflection of the trees in the still waters of the Willamette River.

I sat down in what I have grown fondly of calling my "Beauty and the Beast" chair. Others simply call it a winged back chair. All the same, it was a special chair. It is in this chair that I had devoted nearly a decade of time learning how to quiet my mind. I just could never quiet my mind and do what "they" told you to do. I never quite got the results "they" talked about. This morning was different.

While I didn't get the magic of meditation, I always welcomed the process. I would sink into the cushion of my chair and feel my body relax and ease so deeply into the comfort of my perch. After taking a deep breath or two, as I had done for years and years, I gave thanks for the peace of mind I had and the grace that I felt from the silence. This natural high was beyond measure. I sank even further into the cushion, my arms resting on the armrests. I found myself drifting away and then, without warning, I heard a voice ever so clearly say, ***"You don't need to own to enjoy."***

"What?" I said out loud as I opened my eyes in surprise. "Did I really hear that? Where did that come from? Was I making that up? Was that really me that said that?"

But it couldn't have been, I reasoned. I don't talk like that. I wouldn't say, "You don't need to own to enjoy." That was like a foreign language to me in many ways. "Wow," I thought. "I think I just heard my 'Inner Voice' speak to me for the first time. But what does that mean?" As a realtor, that is a foreign concept; realtors live for owning real estate—lots of it. They live to purchase, to possess, to hold indefinitely. Why would I ever consider letting go of my need to own? That is a way of life for me. Those words I heard were nonsense. Or were they? I struggled with it because I truly believed they came from somewhere special. Consider it God speaking or my intuition or my Inner Voice or my natural knowing. It did not matter. I had come to a place in my life where it didn't really matter what I called it. I just believed there was this Universal Energy that had some play in our lives. Other than that, I don't think I had it clearly defined. All I knew that morning is that "it" was divinely delivered and I couldn't dismiss it.

But unfortunately, I did. Over the years I recalled these words as if they were my mantra but I put no thought into honoring what it meant. I let it go and went on with my life without any regard to those calming words that came that crisp fall morning. Perhaps more than a year went by, and I don't recall ever having the same experience as I did that morning. Although I religiously climbed into my Beauty and the Beast chair and quieted my mind, I fell short of that eventful experience. Never once have I discounted it as "real" or "without purposeful intent" but I struggled for years with the hope of a second coming… until one night, after everyone had gone to bed. I sat in my chair and asked, "Why have I not heard anything since?" I became frustrated and began to demand an explanation. I expressed my doubt. I confessed that I questioned the validity of God or the ability to hear the guiding voice that I believed resided within each of us. Again, without warning, a voice, as I can best describe it, cried out with matched frustration, *"Because you don't listen."*

"I don't listen!" I challenged. "Of course I listen. I sit and listen, but I don't hear anything."

"Because you don't listen," these words repeated. It was as if I was having a conversation with myself. I spoke my words and the words I heard back were clear and immediate. It was unlike any other experience I had had. This voice was a part of me but it was a separate part of me. It felt like it came from within but had this indescribable detachment. It wasn't like the times I talk to myself to build my confidence or motivate myself before an event. It was like another person inside of me.

I know that sounds strange but that is the only way I can describe it. This voice came from a place deep inside me that spoke to me as if it were a close friend or a loving parent. So I decided to give up the fight and surrender to it all and go with the flow. Okay, this voice wants to have a conversation with me so I will accept the invitation.

"So why do you think I don't listen?"

"Because you don't."

"I'm sorry, I have spent most of my life trying to listen."

"And you hear only what you want to hear."

"What does that mean?"

"You hear only what you are comfortable hearing."

"I don't get it. What do you want me to do?"

"What have we told you over and over again?"

"I don't know. What?"

"Write."

"Write? What do you mean, write?"

"Go write."

At this point I had to agree that I had received all types of nudging, pushing, encouraging, suggesting, offering invitations to write. I didn't act on it because, looking back, I didn't have the confidence. But hearing this now, I understood the words, "You don't listen" and "you hear only what you are comfortable hearing". The room was silent. It was as if my Inner Voice knew I needed time to reflect.

"So what do you want me to do?" Now testing, "You tell me clearly what you want me to do and I will do it."

Firmly, almost angrily, the voice commanded, *"Go Write!"*

Whoo! I didn't expect that. This voice was acting like it had been telling me for years and had given up several times and now had the opportunity for one last chance and wanted it to be good, like a two by four to the forehead. There was nothing gentle about this one.

This time, the voice rang out, *"Go Write."*

"Go write? Write about what? What am I suppose to write about?"

"GO WRITE."

That could not have been any more commanding, any more affirming. I had barely got to the point of hearing the voice within and it was now shouting at me, scolding me. I better do what it says, I thought, looking around the room for some eerie exorcist sort of experience. So I got up and went to my computer and sat down at the keypad. As the blank word doc popped up on the screen, I sat there, poised and motionless. I racked my mind for ideas and searched and questioned and finally asked, "What am I supposed to write about?"

"Intuition," came the response without a beat.

"Intuition? What do I know about intuition?"

There was no response.

Intuition? I'm not sure I had ever had that topic come up as a subject I wanted to write about or felt qualified to write about. How can this be right? How could I be asked to write about intuition? So I asked again, "I don't know anything about intuition. How am I supposed to write about that?"

There was no response. The voice was gone now. I was supposed to write. I was accused of not listening. So I was going to write by golly about intuition. I placed my fingers on the key board and for the longest time I just sat. And I sat. Within my mind raced random thoughts from "Who am I to write about intuition" to "This is ridiculous, absurd, a waste of my time." The internal struggle was daunting. I had this incredible experience that lifted me off my chair and marched me across the room to my computer and I was fighting it the whole way. I finally closed my eyes and just trusted the words would flow...and they did. I wrote until the early morning hours. I reread it. Some of it seemed pretty profound and other parts sounded like gibberish. "After all," I questioned, "who am I to think I am Holy enough to write about a topic like this?" What an inflated ego I must have.

It wasn't too much time after that experience that I allowed my rational, reasonable mind to convince me that this was all bunk. This was my ego wanting me to be special, to be enlightened, to be gifted. And after all, I was just an ordinary man without the gift of intuition. I abandoned my routine of meditation. My guilt ran rampant over the next four to five years each time I pulled myself to sit quietly in hopes I would hear that faithful voice just one more time. I found myself apologizing for the absence and asking for forgiveness in the same breath I asked for validation. "Just send me a sign so I know you are real," I requested.

Always testing, I wanted proof of the existence of this quiet voice. All was quiet. Such a void in my life. Guilty once more, I realized that my belief was shaken as I only sought refuge when I was in a moment of need. If I truly believed, I would seek this voice even in the moments of exhilaration and happiness. Rarely did I seek to listen to the voice when my life was working well. I didn't need it. I only needed the reassurance when I was troubled and seeking help. The years past and the voice lay dormant until tragedy struck.

It was one of those beautiful fall days in Oregon when the leaves were brilliant colors of orange, yellow and brown. I was driving my children to school when I drove past this property I hadn't noticed before. It sat down off the road surrounded by a bank on three sides. Down in the midst of nine feet of blackberries sat a small cabin with a blue tarp on its roof. There was something about this property that caught my attention. I turned to my kids and said, "I'm going to buy that property."

I later returned and crossed a rickety wooden foot bridge over a narrow creek and cut my way through the overhanging blackberry bushes along a foot-wide dirt path. Once I entered the path, I was unable to see in any direction except for five feet in front of me and from where I came. I trusted I was doing the right thing. I reached the small cabin. The front porch was leaning to one side due to the dry rot of the posts and cross beams. The front door had a broken window and a padlock for securing the home.

I knocked. I knocked again. I was about ready to leave when the door opened, and in front of me stood an elderly man with nothing on other than a long white t-shirt. I inquired if he was the owner. He confirmed he was with a confused response. "Why?" he asked.

"I was wondering if you had ever considered selling your property?"

"Maybe. Who are you?"

"I live up the street and I have driven by your property for some time and thought it was a cool piece of property."

"Go ahead and look around. I don't mind." He turned back inside and closed the door.

That was odd I thought. Look around? How was I supposed to do that with a wall of blackberries everywhere you looked? I grabbed a broom stick off his porch and started beating down the blackberry bushes around the side of his house. To my surprise the creek appeared in the near distance. How could that be? The creek was back there. Oh, my gosh, is it possible the creek starts up there and comes down the ravine and circles around the house like a horseshoe and comes back to where I crossed the bridge? This property was more magical than I had ever imagined. A rush ran through my body. I determined I had to have this property.

It took me six months, countless idle conversations on his front porch and several random meetings at our favorite neighborhood coffee shop to give John Moses enough time to let go of his hermit house and move to an apartment he'd rented downtown several months before.

First thing I did was hire a crew to take all the berry bushes down. Amazing. The property came to life. It was magical. You could now see how the creek meandered through the property past the house and circled around the curved bank that climbed fifty feet for total privacy. It continued past a beaver dam and circled back towards the road, under a culvert and dumped out on the other side working its way down to the Tualatin River. A stand of bamboo perched itself on the bank of the creek just across from the house. Often, on a sunny day, I would walk down to this magical property and sit. I would sit and sit. It was a beautiful place. The energy was amazing.

My original concept of a cabin grew in to a dream home beyond measure. Nine months went by. They were challenging months. We had seen months and months of rain. I had never built a home before but I learned the painstaking demands of constructing a 3200-square-foot home and separate guesthouse in the dead of winter. By the end of the process the builder didn't like me much and I can't say I cared for him either. It represented a period of time in my life that I devoted much of my days to visiting the site to make sure things were done correctly. So many decisions to make. So many hours committed to this project of love. When they say your home is your castle, they were right about this one. I invested over a year to get this palace built to my liking and on that Mother's Day weekend in May of 2007 when we moved in, I felt like a King overlooking my Kingdom.

Nearly a year had passed. When the weather turned for the better in March, we began to move our living to the outdoors. We returned to the bonfire pit we had built the year before and we once again began to entertain. Our home, fondly referred to as "The Cabin" was the first choice for a "hang out" for my children and their friends. Countless evenings were spent with a round of bodies dipping their smore sticks into the fire and laughing joyously at the simpleness of life. Often, mornings would bring a dozen or so bodies sprawled out on the sectional and across the floor. The home was well loved and the happiness was apparent.

One morning I sniffed. Something was odd. I sniffed again. It was on my clothes. I went to my closet. The smell seemed to be strongest in the closets. I was curious but not alarmed. Not alarmed until days later, a contractor friend of mine came over and within minutes said, "Mark, you have mold." Mold? I ordered a test. The results were conclusive. I had high levels of mold on all three floors. This couldn't be. My castle was ridden with mold. It hit me. The builder framed the house in the dead of winter and never dried the wood. During construction, when I questioned the wet floors, he brushed it off. Now, nine months after moving in, we were confronted with the infestation of mold. I ordered yet another physical inspection that required my removing the speakers from the ceilings and permitting them to cut into my walls. The result: mold was rampant and would require gutting the entire house to treat the infected wood that supported the walls to my castle. What did all this mean? Could the news be any worse? I realized I had hit bottom. Or, had I?

My daughter began to show signs of a soar throat and a runny nose within minutes of entering the house. My chest felt congested and I felt sluggish a good portion of the time. The hygienist and others recommended that it was not healthy for us to remain in the house. My son suggested getting a military tent to move into for a short time. We searched the internet and by ten o'clock the next morning we had a 20 by 40 foot military tent raised in our back yard. As I threw pillows and blankets from the third floor windows, my children and their friends carried our furniture and bedding to our new home. After all, this would be a fun experience. At one end we had three queen beds. At the other, we had our living room with our overstuffed leather couches and electricity running to the TV and DVD player since we had no cable to the tent. It seemed like the right thing to do, especially since the kids were so intrigued with the idea.

The novelty wore off in less than three months. By now I had hired an attorney and the news was not good. I was warned the court battle could last twelve to eighteen months. The estimates to correct the construction defects were now reaching nearly twice what I paid to have the house built. I was informed it would be better to burn my house down and build it back. How could this be? The reality that I might lose my house was becoming a modern day twilight zone.

The cold, wet winters of Oregon were approaching. I needed to accept the inevitable. I needed to abandon my home. As our moving date became closer, I took walks around the property and throughout the house and recalled the many memories. My mind took me to parties we once had, the cuddling with my children on the couch we treasured so dearly, the laughter, the creating, the bonding. And now, it was slipping through my fingers. Not just an ordinary home, I had dreams of creating a retreat center on this magical property. It was ripped away from my reality. "This is too brutal to be just a lesson. This is a redirection, big time." On that day, I let it all go. I released everything over to a Universal Energy that I believed always works for our highest good. I began my journey of surrendering on a day-by-day basis, never knowing where this was going to heal me.

The pictures on the walls seemed all so temporary at this point, the love and the commitment to designing this perfect home seemed so wasted and meaningless, the hopelessness and despair caught up with me and I fell to my knees and wept. My jaw tightened, the tears streamed down my face, my body huddled on the floor, the pain so deep, the sadness so great; "Why this?" I cried.

A faint, soft voice spoke, "*You don't need to own to enjoy.*"

IN SEARCH OF
THE ELUSIVE TRUTH

When we tap into it,
there is a wealth of knowledge
far beyond our own understanding.

Somewhere along the way, I decided I wanted to hear the voice within. I think it started when I was in my late twenties. I had participated in many "personal growth seminars" and my eyes were opened. I remember thinking that "now that I have experienced this level of awareness, I can't go back to my old way of thinking." Even though I knew that way of thinking was easier and this new awareness was more challenging at best.

What was that old way? It was clouded with black and white thinking, with victim thinking, with placing the blame on others when I wasn't really prepared to take responsibility myself. In fact, back then, I'm sure I didn't consider the notion that there was an energy field that is influenced by our thoughts and actions; I didn't take responsibility for my thoughts and how my reality was created by the law of attraction.

Instead, I spent a good bit of time focusing on repelling that which I didn't want instead of focusing on that which I did want. It was an easier way of thinking because it was based on simple principles. I looked at life with a clear understanding of what was right and what was wrong, what was good and bad. I relied only on myself for the decisions and actions I would act upon. I didn't believe that there was a force much greater than myself. I didn't understand that we hold a resource deep within us that opens the doors to greater awareness and understanding.

There is this intelligence within us, dormant at times, ready to be unleashed and acted upon. I came to know this energy, this essence, as the Universal Energy. That it was in us and all around us. When we tap into it, there is a wealth of knowledge far beyond our own understanding. I came to understand there is a Spiritual Intelligence, an essence, an energy that resides within me. This Spiritual Intelligence or Inner Voice, as I refer to it, became my journey in life.

I cannot define this concept of Universal Energy and how it relates to our Inner Voice. It would be like trying to explain what our soul looks like. Is it a shadow, an invisible image of our self, a being of some kind? I do not know. It represents an essence, an energy field of some kind. It isn't solid nor liquid. It just is.

It is like a dense fog that is everywhere. It is the magic that surfaces with coincidences, the indescribable connection with people or places, the blessings of peace and joy. It is what people refer to as being "in the zone" where things just rhythmically happen with ease of effort. It is the beauty around us and the wonderment of life. I cannot explain it exactly. But at some level, we have all experienced it. The unusual, the supernatural, the unexpected.

It is those times when we ask, "How did that just happen?" Something far greater than our self is at work. Something is creating this around me and I can't fully explain it. The Universal Energy or Spiritual Intelligence is all around us and it comes through us.

We don't notice it because we are often too busy with the world around us. The chatter. The noise. When we quiet our mind, we are able to catch a glimpse of it. Tapping into this Universal Energy as it passes in and through us is expressed to us as our Inner Voice. We are able to close off our other senses when we are in the meditative state so that we are able to hear what we might not otherwise have heard. The Inner Voice is simply an expression of the Universal Energy as we come to know it through our awareness.

With my awareness came a desire to search for more, search for a greater understanding of life and why we are here. What is our destiny? What is our purpose? What is this power of the mind they talk about? What is this voice that they refer to at the heart chakra level? I was more than curious, I was committed. In an unconscious way, I began my search for "the deeper meaning." That "deeper meaning", however, was elusive. What does that mean? I had opened the door and now it was impossible to go back.

Over the years I have expressed these sentiments to many people that had just encountered their "awakening" and they felt the same way. They could relate to the fact that they knew something was different, they were exposed to something just out of reach and they were committed to finding out what that was. They too had experienced the notion of "what if there is something more?" When you come from the practical, reasonable mind that has order for everything, it is unsettling when you consider that there may be something out there in the unknown that guides us more than we know. Certainly religion or spirituality has suggested that there is a Higher Power "out there" beyond our bodies. This notion that a spirit or a God guides and directs our lives. But what if this "external" power is not guiding our life? What if there is some force within us? After all, how could God have the ability to reach down into everyone's life and make a difference? How is it possible for this external force to control our destiny? Whether for good or bad, are we claiming from a spiritual perspective that it manifests from a source outside our body?

That's how I grew up. I grew up believing that God was something out there. God had influence and power over us from the bleachers on the sidelines. Prayer was directed out there to a source beyond, not knowing exactly what that was. I don't ever recall growing up hearing a prayer that talked about what was inside each and every one of us. It was a prayer "asking" for assistance from a source that somehow had the power to deliver. I remember as a child believing you had to kneel by your bed at night when you wanted to pray. The focus of my attention was never towards my inner soul but outwards to the sky. My prayers were directed to an entity outside myself. I often wondered how this entity had the ability to respond to all of my requests.

When I look at many modern religions of today, I continue to see the focus outside the body. It is directed with uplifted arms or bent knees to something out there and certainly seeking guidance and direction from an entity beyond the pews. It was the introduction of New Thought Religions that opened my eyes back in those young adult years. It was that commitment to searching for the truth that I discovered a whole new way of thinking...or believing. It was hard for me to accept that there was a possibility that God, a Higher Power, the Universal

Energy, (whatever you want to call it) resided within me and had the influence over my life which I handed over to this external source all those years. It was troubling and scary for me to think that I, as an ordinary man, had this gift of Source within Me. That was too awesome a responsibility. That meant that I had to take full responsibility of my life. I had to come to grips with the fact that the guiding principle in my life was not outside but rather it was within me.

Having come from a strongly indoctrinated religion that promoted an external God, I almost felt guilty when I believed my God was Me. I think I pushed away my search for a deeper meaning because of fear and guilt. "Who am I?" I asked myself over and over again. "Who am I to think that I have the Source within and it is simply a process of learning how to access it." Remember, I was still living in a world that reached "out" to God. Meditation was a freaky thing back then. Certainly, I would never allow myself to be seen looking within. The thought of it alone made me uncomfortable. I would sneak away to a quiet place, hoping no one would discover me "looking within". At some level, I thought it suggested I was "off" in some unusual or unstable way- looking for the lost soul.

That internal search was definitely not main street when I was in my early years developing my beliefs about the God within. While the notion of meditation has become more accepted, I think it is safe to say that our society, as a whole, still questions the concept of controlling our destiny by the choices we make from the guidance taken from Spirit residing within us.

I'm not talking about rational decisions that come from our mental processes. I'm talking about acting on the "guidance" from a Source still undefined by many. It is reasonable to suggest that a great number of people would shudder if they heard someone say, "I was guided to act in that way." The notion that people are guided by an external force may be questioned by some yet the thought of being guided from an Inner Voice might be interpreted by most as psychotic. That is just too freaky.

I think even those that believe that God resides within each and every one of us hesitates when they consider the authenticity of actions taken by guidance within. There is a degree of doubt when someone claims to have taken action by the voice that spoke to them. We have been so tainted by those spiritual leaders who claimed their specialness by asserting they "heard the voice of God." They have wanted to separate themselves by suggesting they have something the rest of us do not. This "gift" is therefore questioned each time it has been professed.

Suppose, however, that this "gift" is demystified by asserting that each and every one of us has this gift, this ability. It does not take place with the few at the podium when they claim their Godlike qualities. How could we challenge this gift of Inner Knowing, this God-given Skill of tapping into our "internal God" if we all demonstrated it equally? No one gets too excited when someone claims a gift of music, a talent for art, or the brilliance of an impressive mind. No, that is reasonable. That is common. That is attainable. But tapping into the power of the Inner Voice and commanding an abundant life by acting on what you hear, that is far too improbable.

It is more likely to assume that it is easier to stumble along, ask for forgiveness, and demonstrate your faith by searching for direction from someone, something other than ourselves. After all, it would require far too much accountability if we could have the power to tap into a knowledge base that could guide us more effectively. I think we are primarily lazy. We again and again take the route that may not serve us for our highest good because it is easier.

Taking the responsibility of doing what's right, that which we know to be the most honorable thing, requires too much effort. When we don't hold the responsibility of our actions to the gate keeper of our soul, then we don't have to make good choices, do the right thing, take the high road. We pick and choose. We analyze it and make a mental decision with what we think is best and often that means passing on the more challenging path choice because it requires courage and faith and ownership to stay the course. We pick and choose what we like best. We pick and choose what is easier. We pick and choose what avoids pain.

That is both the blessing and the curse of listening to the truth of the Inner Voice. There is no picking and choosing. There can't be. If the power of that Inner Voice is so true, then we must honor what we hear and act on it at all times. We don't have the luxury of picking and choosing. Listening and responding to that which comes, regardless of the fears, requires a tremendous amount of courage and faith.

How often are we projecting our prayer requests to the external world and responding to the results that come our way? I sometimes feel that the results from someone's willfull outward request is simply applying the law of attraction… and a lot of faith. Thinking about something long enough and focusing on it with enough faith, it is likely that you might get what you wished for. My struggle with that is that I can't help but believe the ego kicks in. Our Hidden Agenda steps in. Our mind has blinders that takes in what it wants and screens it and releases it through filters. Having passed through these filters, our perceptions can be skewed drastically. What we see and what we want or what we need can be completely different from what is right for us. The voice within is truly like a gate keeper to our soul. It is the monitor of our faith and our fiction. It is the unbiased mediator that knows the truth. It is the quiet voice that reminds us of the integrity of surrender and the passion for what is right.

Many Christians speak of surrendering to God. They talk about turning it over to God. To me that is like the giving over a part of your source, your guiding energy. When you turn it over to God, that again is an outward projection. It is releasing it to some space and energy outside of our bodies. Why not hold onto that Energy Source in full? Grounded and whole, the voice within is powerful and plentiful. Turning it over to God suggests to me that a portion of you, a portion of your essence is handed over, is relinquished when it is directed outside of yourself.

My visual is seeing the spirit, your pure essence passing from your body over to the void. Because where does it go? When you surrender it outside of yourself, where does it go? You are relinquishing a portion of who you are over to a portion of who you are not. By reflecting within, by deepening the awareness within yourself, you are seeking the truth, the core of your ever-waking spirit, to call upon and allow it to resonate. Surrender within. Surrender all that you know and all that you try to make happen to the soft, gentle voice within. Release expectations of the Inner Voice and surrender to what comes forth from the wealth of wisdom and knowing from within.

If you have ever had a problem and you have a loyal friend who asks you about your thoughts or feelings, with every question you go deeper to the truth. You delve down deeper with each inquisition. You search the reservoir of your mind and spirit and heart. You pull back more and more layers of the onion until you get to the core and discover the real truth, often times quite different from what you originally thought. We search, we ask, we consider, we ponder from within. When asking those compelling questions for a deeper truth, we don't seek "outside"; we search within. When the awakening occurs, the "ah-ha" happens, we feel truth, we know truth. It has been likened to a "light going on." A pearl of wisdom. Absolute clarity.

Why not consider this is the same process, the same reasoning behind the Inner Voice knowing all. By tapping into the depths of our Inner Voice, we seek the truth and we discover the knowing. That is why it is often referred to as "our natural knowing."

A PRACTICE OF BEING

The next time you pray, notice where your thoughts and energy are focused. Is it directed to something, somewhere outside the body? If so, move your attention back inside while you continue your same practice of prayer. See if you notice a difference when your prayer is directed inward.

Who is this voice?
Is it always right and serve us in our highest potential?
Is it the voice of God or a voice that comes within?
A messenger of the past and personal guide for our future.
To determine our own futures
Is it a carryover from previous lives that reminds us of our mistakes
and takes us to a place of better understanding and growth?

January 26, 2002
From The Author's Journal

If our bodies have the ability to feel a wound, sense danger, read minds,
die and send a soul somewhere,
why can't our bodies possess the powers otherwise attributed to God?
Is this universal energy an energy attributed to an entity
that exists out there or could this energy be a part of the human anatomy.
The power of this controlling energy is within each of us,
like the pounding of our heart.
We are in control and we have the power
by tuning into the power within.

January 28, 2002
From The Author's Journal
The Inner Voice

PERSONAL INSIGHTS

PERSONAL INSIGHTS

UNIVERSAL ENERGY
& ALLOWING IT TO FLOW

*When we align our will
with the will of our Universal Energy,
miracles happen.*

Perhaps the most frequently asked questions I hear in my workshops are "What is the Inner Voice?", "What does the voice sound like?" and "How will I know when I hear it?" You will just know. I have heard, "the tone is different" or "it's not the way I talk" or "it comes from a different part of my body" or "it comes from my heart and not my head" and on and on and on. It's different for each person.

I explain it as a voice that doesn't place blame or guilt. There is no judgment. It is not a voice that infers a sense of obligation or responsibility. It is a very forgiving voice; it is a nudge that is reassuring and comforting. It doesn't suggest sensibility of command but a command for sensibility. There is this quality of ease and acceptance.

Although the message may be overwhelming and challenging at times, it does not pressure or try to persuade you. It is a sense of "knowing" that can't be explained. We may not like what we hear but we know what we hear makes sense. It resonates with us. It speaks to us in a humble and reassuring way that opens up a part of us that is responsive to listening, however unsettling it might be. I am always grateful, regardless of the message. When the ego speaks, I often feel a sense of obligation which doesn't always feel right. When the ego speaks, it frequently sounds self-serving while the Inner Voice speaks routinely in service to others. The ego speaks from the mind, the Inner Voice is more of an inspiration.

Where does inspiration come from? Hard to tell. It is similar to the origin of the Inner Voice. Inspiration comes in thoughts, actions, feelings, words, images. So does the Inner Voice. It comes to each of us in very different ways. Over time, it is our duty to determine how it speaks to us by evolving our practice of quieting the mind and allowing it to flow.

What is this flow? What is this Inner Voice? Does it really matter? Too often we want to know the answers. We want to know exactly what something looks like or feels like. "Dad, tell me what love feels like." It is difficult to explain until you have experienced it for yourself. If you developed a practice of quieting your mind and listening for the Inner Voice and it guided you to some incredible experiences, would you care what it was called or what it looked like? Was it God? Was it my intuition? Was it my Inner Voice or my Higher Power? Does it really matter? I can share with you my thoughts but, again, being redundant, does it really matter?

I use many of these words loosely. One means the other. They are exchangeable. I could use God for Universal Energy and visa versa. I use Inner Voice for Natural Knowing. I call the spirit that resides in each and every one of us as our Higher Power. They are interchangeable. The one means them all. I believe there is a Higher Power or a Universal Energy that is all around us and runs through us. This energy field or essence or presence is interconnected with all things. It connects the flow of nature, our thoughts and our feelings, our actions, our place on this earth. I think this concept is described in *The Lion King* when they say "the circle of life." What starts out comes around to a completion or an end. There is no break in the loop. It is connected. It continues. It completes the cycle. It is further illustrated with the Law of Attraction. The fact that we can focus on something and draw the energy towards us and create that which we are seeking. What is that energy? What is that power? The Power of the Mind? The Higher Power? A little bit of both? Perhaps they are connected.

The Science of Karma suggests that there is a relationship between "cause and effect". That there is this idea that everything that surrounds us is interconnected in causal chains that are not always obvious or apparent. They just are. Events or happenings are all connected and come together at some point as the effect of our causing them by thought or action. Life is in equilibrium, in balance.

When out of balance, the equilibrium (or Karma, The Higher Power, God, Universal Energy) brings it back into balance. The interconnectedness of the Universal Energy keeps everything in check. What effects one thing, effects another. It is interconnected and yet it is embodied. It is within the bubble or dispersed amongst the mist. There is a link for everyone and every thing just like a puzzle. A place for every piece. When we can find our rightful place in the order, we complete the whole.

When we align our will with the will of our Universal Energy (Higher Power, Inner Voice), miracles happen. We are dancing through life with rhythm and grace. We are appreciative of what is happening in our lives. Our Higher Power wants us to find our place and it is when we are able to tap into our will and unite it with the will of this Universal Energy, miracles happen. Peace of mind. Harmony in the world. Abundance and Grace. Happiness and Success.

The alignment occurs most frequently by quieting the mind or through meditation when we are able to circumvent the filters and the blindfolds of the mind that prevent us from taking rightful ownership in our place with the Universal Energy. With old habits and beliefs that prevent us from stepping fully into who we are, these filters prevent us from creating synergy with our Higher Power or the Universal Energy.

When the alignment is strong and our world is celebrating our place on the conveyor belt of life, then we need to surrender and accept what is. This rightful place can be reinforced by simply expressing gratitude. Acknowledge your rhythm and your coincidences. Give thanks to the people that come to serve you and those that support you. Be appreciative of the abundance that comes your way. Allow it to flow. Welcome it. Expect it.

God wants us to experience great things. God wants us to live our authentic journey because when we do, we serve mankind.

So whatever you want to refer to it as, this Power, this Essence wants for us to be happy and live our authentic journey. In its purest form, it wants us to find our place on the path of life. The challenge is finding it at its purest form. That is our journey. That is our destiny. That is the purpose of this book.

A PRACTICE OF BEING

The next time you experience an inspirational thought or what you might consider inspired guidance, follow it and see how it flows. Watch how it evolves. Can you put a place of origin for this inspired guidance? The Source? Then let it all go, and accept that it just comes to you.

What I have discovered is that there is no one mechanism
that connects with you.
There exists an equilibrium between multiple forces
that guides us throughout our life.
I am not sure, and not sure that it matters,
that they are interrelated
or consciously aware of the existence of the others,
but certainly they play off of each other and impact each other.
These related yet unrelated qualities of life
consist of experiences we have
in the physical plane, the mental plane, and the spiritual plane
all connected by a synergistic energy called
the Universal Energy.

April 8, 2008
From The Author's Journal
Personal Insights from a Meditation

PERSONAL INSIGHTS

JUST BE QUIET

When we are quiet,
the body and mind
are brought back into balance.

Have you ever been in a conversation with a person that just doesn't stop talking? You will notice their whole body gets into it. They often use their arms for gestures, their head and eyes are continuously darting from idea to idea. They are so engrossed in talking (which is an outward expression) that they rarely hear or listen to responses (an inward expression). It is as if they have something desperately important that they have to unload or get off their chest. They are unconscious in their communicating because they fail to defer to someone else's comments.

I have a friend like this. She gets on a roll and there is no getting in. I might even say something like, "let me say something" or "can I say something" but it doesn't penetrate her wall of communicating externally. After a while, I just give up trying to communicate with her and I take in what I want and drift off to another place, resolved I'm not going to get a word in. It becomes almost agonizing to sit with someone with such a one-sided conversation. Eventually, I find a way to interrupt the conversation and end it with my departure.

I have friends that are very successful in the corporate world or with their own businesses. They lead very hectic lives. They are always on the go. For them, there is just not enough time in the day. They are grabbing their coffee on the run, returning email from their blackberry, pounding down power lunches before they launch their afternoon agenda.

By the time they get home they are exhausted but that doesn't stop them from the pace they have fallen victim to all day. They might skip the extended welcome with their kids to catch up on business in their home office. Dinner is pleasant but their attention isn't fully there. They spend the evening reviewing documents and stay up late after everyone else has gone to bed. They never stop their forward motion. They are committed to the external drive to push on with their day and get the job done. They are like the Eveready Battery; they just keep on going.

My mind operates at warp speed. I'm always thinking and creating in my mind. I am not alone. I rarely listen to music in the car because I get so caught up with my thinking. I'm always processing. The mind is a beautiful thing and I am not going to waste one minute of its usefulness.

There are millions and millions of other people trapped in their minds just like myself. Their world revolves around a whirlwind of ideas and thoughts. If you listen closely you can almost hear the wheels churning in their head.

This mega machine is their livelihood, their sustenance. It is a powerful device that keeps them being as productive as they are. Thank goodness they were blessed with such an active mind that keeps them on track in a very productive way each and every day. One wonders, however, if it is a blessing or a curse.

Our world is filled with stimuli. Everything is immediate and often without conscious thought. The internet is instantaneous. There is no pulling out the phone book or checking a book out of the library. That takes too long. When we can google and get what we need in minutes, if not seconds, why would we take the unnecessary time to accomplish the same task with old methods of doing things that take longer?

If we can't take a few minutes to walk into the restaurant to get our food, we pull up to a drive through. Coffee huts are springing up all around serving instant coffee without the wait. We pound on the horn if the driver ahead of us hesitates for a split second.

We're on a fast pace that is for sure. But the worst of it is that not only are we on this unconscious pace, more and more things are being done for us without our need to be aware. What's this with automatic flushing devices on the public toilets? I don't have to even think or take any action. I can just walk away.

Have we lost the ability (or desire) to do the mundane tasks of living? We don't have to turn on our car headlights anymore. They go on and off automatically. I don't have to open a door; it opens as I approach. I don't have to recall my password, my computer recalls it and logs me in. And this one drives me mad: we don't have to carry on a conversation, we can just text each other.

Our world is moving faster and faster with technology and gadgets that remind us of the importance of speed at the cost of being consciously aware. Our children have succumbed to the numbing effect of speed and disconnectedness. They want to be instantaneously entertained with the luxury of a broadcast text to their friends for the latest itinerary of events planned for the evening.

No wonder employers complain about this Millennial Generation not having good interpersonal communication skills… they never had to develop them. Perhaps some day the countertops of our customer service departments will be equipped with personal hand held devices on a chain so the customer can receive the text from the employee across the counter.

We as a society have become more and more disengaged with our internal world. We are lost in our fast paced society, our gadgetries of the day, our satiation with our self, and a new-found laziness that requires less and less from us each day. If we are not careful, we will become less aware of our surroundings and oblivious of ourselves.

This preoccupation with "stuff" out there is taking us away from the great "stuff" that lies within us. The more we focus on activities out there, the less we will focus on the phenomenal activities that are bubbling up within. The host of miracles that rests quietly within represents the dormant opportunities that each of us have available to us to live a life more thrilling than the high we achieve from the latest video game.

In many ways we have lost our connection with the inner world and our deepest reservoir of the self-actualized soul. From the self-indulged communicator to the fanatical career-minded individual that believes it is all about doing, and finally to those that are so absorbed in their minds, they all need to be reminded to "BE QUIET".

Listening to your Heart:
Finding out who You are
Is not simple.
It takes time for
The Character to quiet down
In the Silence of the "not doing."
We begin to know
What we feel
If we listen and hear
What is offered.
Then anything in Life
Can be our guide.
Listen!

Author Unknown

It's too easy to say we don't have time, we don't know how, we can't understand this, we won't do that. It's just not a priority. We make stopping at the drive thru on the way to work a priority. Why can't we, why won't we take the same amount of time to "be quiet".

Meditation can be intimidating; quiet time is not. Taking 15 minutes of quiet time each day doesn't require learning specific techniques. Sit quietly in a soft chair after you take your morning shower. When you arrive to work, sit quietly in your car before you jump into the rat race. During your lunch break, find a relaxing place outdoors to sit and hear the beauty of nature all around you. When you are driving in the car or waiting for an appointment, sit quietly without the radio or a nearby magazine. Sit quietly. Rest your body. Rest your mind. Sink into your body and feel your muscles and your limbs relax. Exhale. Direct your attention to your breath and away from your racing mind. Take a deep breath. Relax. Be still. Be quiet.

Don't set any expectations. Don't judge yourself if nothing seems to happen or no change takes place. Be patient and let it unfold in all due time. Taking quiet time will help clear the mind and the results of your discipline might come later in the day or at times when you least expect it.

The Quiet Time allows the body to rebalance itself. When we are moving at an amazing pace, thinking, pushing, always on the go, we don't seem to see the obvious. It is like trying to fit an object in a hole with repeated attempts failing in frustration. When we step back and take the pressure off, the second attempt, without the anxiety, often results in a better perspective and the piece fits perfectly in the hole.

In life, we push and force in our routine of life; when we are quiet, the body and mind are brought back into balance. The quiet time is the time for the mind to rest and the energetic flow in our body to redefine itself from a frenetic pace to a more orderly flow. A calmness comes over our body and for that moment we are free of stress; we continue our day with greater peace.

From a simplistic point of view, how could this place of calmness, without the pressure of stress, be bad for you? Settling the body with repeated inhales and exhales feeds the body with oxygen and nourishes the body with a cleansing of the spirit.

This process of Quiet Time is the simplest, most effective way to rejuvenate the body, mind, and soul. Take the time. Go be it.

A PRACTICE OF BEING

At several points throughout your day, take two to five minutes to focus your attention on things that are pleasant to you and bring you peace. Stop yourself when you find yourself in a frantic pace and find something around you that calms your soul. Whether it be the bright yellow leaf on the maple tree outside your window or the sight of a young child at play or the slapping of the water against the bank of the river or the gentle words of a passing song, take a moment and quiet your mind and let go of your thoughts. What is your experience after you have taken this opportunity to be Quiet?

Unbelievable. What I got loud and clear today was,
'It's not what you have, it's what you do.'
I heard that and wasn't quite sure so I asked what that meant
and the voice came back almost immediately,
'It's not what you possess or own, it's what you do with your life.'
Incredible.
I heard that loud and clear.
It was a knowing.
A spirit within me offering these words to me.

November 5, 2001
From The Author's Journal
Personal Insights from a Meditation

PERSONAL INSIGHTS

LISTENING
COMES IN MANY WAYS

*It will remain silent and still
until you give it an opportunity to speak.*

I learn differently than many people I know. I'm a more visual person. Show me vs. tell me. Demonstrate how to do something rather than give me a manual. While others do very well with verbal instructions or hearing how things are done. Still others have a sense about things. They just have a feeling about it and they are able to get the job done.

The same holds true for methods of quieting the mind. It's all well and fine to say, "quiet the mind," but many people don't understand what that really means. How does one go about that? Surely they can be in a quiet place or listen to some soothing music but they still have a challenge with stopping the mind with updates and reports on the findings of the day. Our world is certainly fast paced and we have lots to think about and react to on a daily basis. So how do we stop this mind chatter and why is it so important? Let's start with why it is so important.

It is estimated that between 92% and 98% of our thinking is in our subconscious. We are unaware of most of the thoughts we have. These unconscious thoughts control who we are and what we do. Whether they are favorable or unfavorable.

As the saying goes, "If we think we can or think we can't, we will". These thoughts are influenced by experiences we have had in the past, criticisms that have been levied against us, beliefs we have formed, friendships we have made, and on and on.

How then, can one survive having genuine thoughts when they are clouded by the perceptions we draw from these experiences? It has been suggested that we are in our purest form when we are born and then over time we become corrupted. As time goes on we take the pure spirit, the genuine heart, the pure essence of our being and we coat it layer by layer with stuff. Similar to a paper mache project, we start with the core and then over time we add more and more layers until the original form is no longer recognizable.

In many ways, that is what happens with us. Over time we realize that we have many layers to the onion that have masked what we really think, who we really are, and what potential we truly possess. It's scary to pull back the layers of the onion. There are tears and pain when we expose our pretenses and the defense mechanisms that have built up over the years as a means of survival, a means of protecting ourselves from the challenges of life, or those apparent challenges that we have formulated in our minds from our beliefs. When we formulate these beliefs or thoughts as a result of our experiences, they are thoughts we have determined as true in our mind.

All of our conditioning comes from our mind. All of our conscious and unconscious thoughts are significantly impacted by the operations of our mind. In order to remove the layers and layers that we covered ourselves with, in order for us to get back to the genuine self, the core essence of who we are, we must either change our mind or circumvent it. Since 92%-98% of our thoughts are in our subconscious, it might be difficult to change those thoughts. We aren't even aware of what they are. Therefore the best alternative is to go around the mind. Quieting the mind shuts it off so we can penetrate through the dominance of the mind and get to the core. It's like driving a spike through a protective shield to get to the core so that we can let some of this innate brilliance come forth.

It is when we circumvent the mind and go directly to our core, our heart, our soul, our essence, our innate knowing, to the Inner Voice, that we hear the truth. We once again are refreshed with the innocence of our youth and the bliss that comes from that innate knowing we had at birth. All things flow from the beginning, from the Source. Getting to our Source, one must fight the downstream currents of our mind to get to the majesty of the Source.

The journey to this Source is a challenging one. Sometimes it takes a lifetime to get there. It is a continual process, an evolution of our spirit. We can make it difficult or we can make it easy. Quieting the mind or meditating is considered the most common way. I have been frustrated over the years when spiritual teachers have suggested a specific way to meditate. That is like the education system deciding that the only way to teach is to hand out a text book. It doesn't work like that.

Quieting the mind and opening to that purity, the natural knowing I refer to as the Inner Voice can come in multiple ways. For some it is through mediation. For others it is sitting in nature. For others, it comes in dreams. And for some, it comes in isolated moments in their daily living. Being conscious to those moments when you feel guided is where it all begins. Don't get wrapped up with the concept that there is a certain way. When you hear the voice, when you feel the nudge, when you are moved to do something perhaps out of the ordinary, take note. Take note of those precious moments when something guides you, something inspires you, something suggests it is coming from a source other than our self.

My mother, Karma, has always joked that her meditation time is when she takes a bath. She might remain in there for over an hour. There is a reason for that. She is in the flow; she is in her groove. She is inspired by what she gains from this quiet time.

I have a friend that finds her inspiration when she goes for a hike in nature. She surrounds herself with conifer trees and a babbling brook and she experiences God.

An associate of mine says she gets her "hits" at various times throughout the day. She might be at a stoplight and find herself fixed on a beautiful oak tree or she might put aside the magazine and take a moment in a waiting room and welcome the presence of the still mind. Her messages come to her randomly throughout her day. She expects it.

Another friend of mine has meditated for nearly forty years when it was a weird thing to do. He received his mantra and he meditates in bed, usually just before going to sleep. It works for him; it could never work for me because I would fall asleep.

Personally, I love what I fondly refer to as my Beauty and The Beast Chair. I don't ever see myself discarding that chair no matter how faded the fabric becomes. And just recently, I discovered a bench out on the bluff overlooking the Columbia River that does something incredible for me. I took a walk one day with my dog, Hallie, along the path around the marina in Jantzen Beach and came upon a single park bench that overlooked the many sailboats and had an incredible view up river of Mt Hood in the distance. I closed my eyes and listened to the flapping of the sails and the lapping of the water against the shore and I was moved. Inspiration came to me more readily than I had ever experienced before. I go back to that bench often and it continues to provide me immediate inspiration like no other place I have found—even my Beauty and the Beast Chair.

The key is being still; being in the silence and allowing your attention to escape the thoughts of your mind and focus on the Inner Source where the quiet, gentle voice can be heard. When you are at peace, it allows the voice to speak more freely. When you quiet the chatter of the mind or the outside noises, the voice can be heard in the silence.

The Inner Voice does not yell nor does it enter into competition to be heard. It will remain silent and still until you give it an opportunity to speak. It will come forward when you welcome it by preparing your space.

That is why your space, uniquely your own, is so important. When you find the space that works for you, you provide the platform for the voice to come forth. You will often hear about the importance of building an altar. That is the same principle. It is simply preparing a place for you to become still, relaxed, and open to the quiet voice within to speak. An altar or a sanctuary is not as important as the concept is. Whether it is the bathtub or the nature walk or the park bench, it makes no difference as long as you resonate with the stillness of the moment.

A PRACTICE OF BEING

Over several months, at different times of the day, take a moment to be still. Find a place where you can relax and be at peace. See if you notice a difference with each new environment. Is one more conducive than another? What makes one better than the other? What elements are present in the location where you seem most relaxed and at peace? See if you can identify some common elements with several different environments or locations and see if you can identify what elements work best for you when you choose to be still and listen.

I lifted my head and leaned back against the chair
and without thinking, I said,
'God, just tell me what I need to know.'
And before I could gather another thought, I heard this soft voice speak,
'You don't need to own to enjoy!'
Wow. That was different.
That had a whole different feel to it. It even sounded different.
Those are not the words I use. And,
it sounds as if they really speak to me. It makes sense right now where
I am in my life. I am overwhelmed.
I truly believe that for the first time, at least that I acknowledged it,
I heard the voice of God.

October 17, 1994
From The Author's Journal
Personal Insights from a Meditation

PERSONAL INSIGHTS

PERSONAL INSIGHTS

GETTING IT RIGHT

Being who we are
and experiencing who we are in the very moment
is what opens the doors to where we are going.

With my years and years of experiencing personal growth workshops of all kinds, one thing became clear: I loved the process. I loved the discovery. I loved the growth that came, the new understanding. I sat witness to many around me that had something I wanted. Something I thought was intelligence. But I learned it wasn't really about their intelligence that intrigued me it was more about their intuition, of sorts. It was their innate ability to pull things out of the hat from almost nowhere.

Where did that knowledge, that understanding come from? I was always intrigued when an instructor was working with someone and asked a question or two and then went off in an entirely different direction that seemed so inappropriate only to find they had "hit it right on the nail." How did they do that? Where did that instinct come from? Where did they acquire this skill? I wanted that skill.

Thus began my search for a deeper understanding of the power of the mind, the soul, or what lies somewhere in between. What I didn't realize was that my search did not require any travel, no costly seminars or lecture series, or trips around the world to spiritual centers. Instead, I launched my own treasure hunt of worldly advice from the learned, searching and exploring out there rather than within. I completed a number of classes at the various churches I attended while growing up. I enrolled in countless seminars from intuition to rebirthing. I convinced myself that if I filled my bookshelf with a great collection of self help books and my car disc player with the latest from Wayne Dwyer, I would find the answers. I found myself with friends who were ten years my senior and, with their breadth of knowledge, I gobbled up every introspective conversation.

During my early adulthood, I was taken under the wing by several "teachers" that exposed me to their philosophies, their retreat centers, their preferred readings, their CD series. I took it all in.

I spent many evenings praying to the skies on a star-lit night parked by the side of the road overlooking the city. I asked for a sign. "Please, show me a sign that I am on the right path." I hungered so much for reassurance, to be acknowledged and validated. At times I received no conformation. At other times, often during moments of dire distress, I witnessed a shooting star or an unusual twinkle in the sky that I considered my sign of validation. For perhaps over ten years I sought to understand and affirm that the path I was taking was the right one. Never once did I look within.

Only until my later years in life was I introduced to religions or philosophies that suggest that God resides within and the power of God is Ours Internally…not eternally. I often wonder if there was a missed translation or the hand of man that transformed the concept of Internally to Eternally. See, I think the notion of "eternally" is again a sense of "out there." It suggests that we will have an eternal life as it progresses forward into the future. It projects a life that is long and an existence that lies ahead of us…out there. Not in the moment. Not here and now.

In this elusive search for something to be understood out there, this concept of internally vs. eternally caught my attention and I couldn't let it go. I began to realize we were a society of "out theres." Focus was on the future. Tomorrow and tomorrow's tomorrow. With internally, we are in the moment. One cannot go within without being here and now. There is no uncertainty because the certainty is that you are now. You are in the moment. You are experiencing life that is ever present. Being here in the moment offers certainty because we are. Being out there suggests uncertainty because it is beyond where we are right now in the moment. I have learned that much of hearing the Inner Voice is placing ourselves in the moment.

Great scholars, teachers, motivational speakers, ministers, and corporate execs often focus on the tasks at hand in preparation for the future. It is about getting from here to there. A forward motion. A process of progressing from where you stand that moment in your body to a future place that is somewhere different. The whole ecology of our existence is to get somewhere… out there. We aren't satisfied with where we are; we are always searching for where we want to go. Everything is outward.

The focus in work, relationships, religion, in self is searching for direction outside of ourselves for a position other than that which we are. Accepting exactly where we are and the perfectness of it eludes many of us. Being who we are and experiencing who

51

we are in the very moment is what opens the doors to where we are going. The attention (intention) however is very different. Instead of focusing out there to where we want to go, focus inside to where we are right now and allow the "where we want to go" to unfold in consecutive moments.

The meditation movement opened the eyes of many and changed the way they looked at time. The introduction of quieting the mind brought people to the present and away from the search for a tomorrow. More and more people became of the moment rather than for the moment. I watched and was intrigued. That looked interesting to me. But it scared me. It scared me because it took me from the norm of reaching out there for concrete evidence.

The validation, the conformation was elusive. How could I know that this inner space would affirm my beingness, let alone my doingness? I didn't hold hope that I would know the difference. I wasn't sure I would recognize the truth from the fiction. The ego from the self. I couldn't trust myself to be honest. There were no safeguards to protect me against myself. It was all up to me. It was individual, it was mine and mine alone. How then would I really know?

Regretfully, I have been in search of my passion and purpose for most of my adult life. Not that that is a bad thing; it is just so unfortunate that I spent so much time searching outside of my own body. It seemed like the right way to go until I tested the waters of inner knowledge. At first it was a curiosity, a novelty and then it grew into something more essential.

Of course, my ego loved the thought of my being so special that I was gifted with the ability to listen to voices, to hear the words of God, to speak of wiser things. But perhaps it was just a sense of loss or fear of not knowing that caused me to seek peace with the miracle of God speaking to me. Wouldn't that put me at ease, I must have thought. I'm sure there were painful times in my life or times that left me in despair and I believed the solution was to be handed the answer. Like a magic pill. Simple enough.

It makes total sense that if I am to step into my higher level of understanding and knowing that it means I should hear "the voice." How does one do that? Meditation? I began my search. I began to read books, attend seminars, listen to CDs. I was in search of the elusive "method" of hearing the voice within. Years went by and one frustrating attempt after another went by. I tried this method, I tried that method. I sat crossed legged. I hummed. I chanted. I called out my mantra with my thumb and second finger in that all-familiar pose of the "Enlightened One." After all that is what a respected spiritual teacher taught me as the most effective way to meditate.

I didn't get it at first because when one CD didn't work, I bought another. They all ended up at a garage sale months later. Nothing worked. Frustrated and feeling inadequate at my abilities to meditate, I gave up. Months turned into years and I was drawn further and further away from my path.

At times I would sit quietly and ask for forgiveness from the Source I thought resided outside my body. I felt unworthy and full of guilt because of my lack of commitment and dedication. My discipline was pathetic, my commitment compromised. I beat myself up for over five years because I just couldn't do it. I just couldn't capture that voice within. Nothing worked so why try any longer. After all, I thought, there were some that had the talent and some that did not. I must be the one that does not have the talent to tap into the Inner Voice. I couldn't stay with it and get the results from the proven methods that had been shared with me over time by those who knew. I didn't have what it takes.

Now, reflecting back, I can't imagine what I was thinking. If I believed that there was this preordained method of achieving enlightenment with meditation, I set myself up for failure. I might as well have planted in my mind that if I sat in a certain way, held my body in a receptive posture, and focused my attention on a mantra, that I would levitate and begin to fly.

That is what I think we have done over the years with the notion of meditation. We have placed such a stigma to its correctness that we have failed to welcome the natural flow that comes to each of us in very different ways. Meditation is not a discipline of structure it is a structure of discipline. It is not about having this specific structure to make it work, it is about having the routine of discipline.

Put away your tapes, your books, your four-part CD, your notes from the meditation perfection seminar and sit quietly for fifteen minutes every day. Let go of structure. Let go of doing it right. It is simply about quieting the mind.

Being in the Silence. Letting your thoughts and your mind go limp. Let go of the pressure to perform or get amazing results. Sit wherever you are comfortable. Lay down if you like. Close your eyes. Leave your eyes open. Cross your legs. Lift them in the air over your head. Face Mecca. Empty the garbage. Build your altar, close your eyes at a red light. Escape to your favorite place in nature. It doesn't matter. Settle in your seat on the bus and be still. It doesn't matter. Be still. Be quiet. Be in the silence. What matters is that you be quiet on a regular basis. Like exercising any muscle, it takes repetition. Relax your body and let your thoughts dissipate. Take a deep breath or two. Let your body sink into the earth upon which your body rests. Let go of getting it right. Be still. Get comfortable with the stillness. Get comfortable with it as a natural part of your day. Get comfortable with it as a journey and you will get there some day and it will be splendid.

A PRACTICE OF BEING

If you find your mind wandering and you are getting frustrated with the process of meditating, try this very simple technique:

Get yourself in a comfortable position. Relax. Take a deep breath and let out a long exhale. Follow your breath as you exhale. Follow your body as it relaxes to the exhale. Notice the focus of the exhale deepening within your body. Put your focus on your lungs and feel them release. Take your focus away from the exhale through your nose or mouth, and redirect it to your lungs, releasing and relaxing within your body. Remain focused on the cavity of your chest as your ribs move inward. Notice your stomach relax. As you exhale and your lungs release and your ribs relax and move inward, follow your breath to the very end. Focus where it reaches that very end point, like a tide the comes in and reaches that critical point when it eases to a stop and then retreats back out to the ocean. Follow your breath to that point. Now focus on that point, that calm spot within your body. Continue to focus on that very end point of your exhale and whenever your mind begins to chatter, take a deep breath and follow the exhale to this point and refocus there. Do this again, and again, and again, and again.

I found that when I am committed
to getting up and sitting quietly in my chair,
taking the two to three deep breaths
and putting myself in a good place
to receive, the messages began to come
more frequently and were more audible.
Why would God act any differently than a good friend?
The more that I explore my relationship with God
and the communication I have with that voice within,
I realize how so simple it really is.
There is no complicated formula
or scientific studies
that need to be made
to understand how it works and why.

December 11, 2001
From The Author's Journal
Personal Insights from a Meditation

PERSONAL INSIGHTS

PERSONAL INSIGHTS

NO PICKING & CHOOSING ALLOWED

Thoughts of doubt or fear
come into significant play
when acting upon that quiet, unassuming Inner Voice.

I have to plead ignorance to my awareness that over the years I have artfully picked those guiding words I wanted to hear and passed on the words that were packed with fear or resistance. I thought I did a good job of listening and acting on what I heard but it has become quite obvious that I have taken the safe route by responding to that which I was comfortable and pushing aside that which appeared unreasonable or unattainable. If what I heard was safe or within my comfort zone, I would choose to act upon it. However, if I heard something that forced me to stretch, I would frequently justify the irrationality of it and not take action towards it. I was comfortable with ignoring that which brought me stress.

It's easy to argue with yourself or defend your reasoning for going in a certain direction when it is the most logical. It is the illogical guidance that causes us to doubt and convince ourselves that another direction is more appropriate. In truth, it was the rationalization of my ego, attempting to make the road ahead free of bumps and potholes. Regardless of this safeguard, they come anyway.

What I have learned in a very powerful way is that you can't pick and choose what you respond to. You must act on that which you hear, regardless of the fear associated with it. It may bring up hesitation or doubt if you begin to rationalize that it is too impractical or that the task is too daunting. I've realized that when I have put myself in that quiet place and have heard the Inner Voice speak to me, I have chosen to take issue with that which I was uncomfortable and elected, instead, to move forward with another option that made "sense" to me.

It never ceases to amaze me how we justify our decisions on reasoning when, in truth, they are often based on fear. Thoughts of doubt or fear come into significant play when acting upon that quiet, unassuming Inner Voice.

That which we have an investment in can often be the most alarming for us. There is more weight on it because of fear of success or fear of failure. It is far more scary for us to stretch ourselves into doing what we really want to do because we anticipate that we might have to face the truth that we are not good at it or we might fail at our attempt. Facing that truth with that which we act upon can and does often convince us that a safer alternative may be more pleasing. We might act on that which we feel we have more experience or confidence in because the fear of failure may not be as great. So when we get the nudge to act on a life-long dream, the "issues" come up and we choose to stay with the status quo. Again and again, we push aside our passion for something with which we are more familiar.

I have repeatedly heard a voice that encouraged me to take a path that was foreign to me and repeatedly I responded with, "Who am I?" or "What do I know about this?" or "How can I make any money at this?" or "What if I take a run at this and

I fail?" The list goes on and on. At some level, each attempt to reach for my bliss by listening to the voice within has been met with resistance. I can recall numerous times, too many to count, coming out of a meditation and negating what I heard and replacing it with logical arguments that suggested I "pass" on that idea. It was far easier for me to look into my future and predict success with that which I knew I could deliver with confidence. It was always difficult for me to see clearly my path or the outcome I wanted when I was introduced to a new direction that was foreign in conceptualization but true to my heart.

You would think that if I had passion for this guidance, I could see the outcome clearly and be excited about acting on it. I found the reverse to be true. It was almost as if I was directed to go in an entirely new direction and away from the intended goal or objective. I knew the familiar was possible and I could see the steps to get there.

With the implementation of an uncomfortable path, I struggled again and again with the mechanics of getting there. I was challenged with the steps I needed to take and being able to visualize success at the end of the tunnel. The fact is that my mind took over and invalidated my experience and replaced it with what it knew. It required a greater leap of faith to act on that which I had passion for and to let go of old thoughts, beliefs and habits than to step comfortably into that which I knew and presented less stress in my life. That is why many of us pick and choose. We pick that which we believe is easier to manifest and we discard that which is hard to visualize, regardless of how important it is for us to make the shift.

I believe that occurs because of several reasons. We come into this life with a concept of what we think our life will be like. We grow and experience life and over time it molds us into thinking our lives are going to be a certain way. Deviation from that is often difficult. Society plays a huge role in how we think and how we perceive "success" in our lives. For men, it might be the money they make, the status they hold, the recognition they receive, the accomplishments they can report. For women, it might be the home they create, the personal success they achieve, the independence they prove, the equality they attain.

Regardless of this notion, breaking that attachment to the world we think we want can be challenging. Letting go of what we believe is important and stepping into a new world that contradicts or suggests uncertainty can throw anyone into resistance. This resistance is what prevents us from hearing the voice within because we fear we might have to let go of what we know (in our minds).

I think our society has done us all a great disservice by placing so much negativity on the notion of failure. Failure is the greatest gift we have. It holds such a stigma, yet it is so liberating. Imagine the excitement, the adventure, the thrill in life if you could act on what you wanted and fail miserably without judgment. Imagine how freeing that could be in all the decisions you made if you could fail eight out of ten times and go back for more.

Failure is an opportunity for learning and re-adjusting how you look at future adventures before you. When we let go of the fear of failure and willingly step into the unknown by listening and acting upon our Inner Voice, we are truly liberated to live the life we are destined to live. Without the guilt and thoughtful deliberation, we can throw caution to the wind and go for it. When we have a healthy perspective on failure, that release allows us to listen more closely to what we hear and be willing to act on it because the success or failure from the choices we make are insignificant.

Most people want to know where they are heading and where they are going to end up. In order to accomplish that, there must be order and reason. Often, the Inner Voice provides neither. The practical can be placed nicely in a box and the outcome can be articulated. With the Inner Voice there comes a level of uncertainty that requires a generous portion of faith.

Stepping into your willingness to respond to the Inner Voice requires you to step into a world of trust. There usually isn't a clearly defined outcome and there is no road map. With a commitment to follow the voice within, you must have the courage and strength to respond to what you hear without the reassurance that you know what exactly is going to happen. You must have faith that it will unfold perfectly. You cannot change course because you begin to feel fearful because the uncertainty is too great.

That is the power of listening to the Inner Voice; it requires you to step into the depths of the unknown and trust that the next step will be provided to you in perfect timing. Surrendering is not enough. It requires much more than the notion of surrendering. With surrendering, you must welcome that something better is going to happen. With surrendering, you must partner with optimism and faith. Welcome in the notion of Faith and attract positive outcomes by being ever-so-present with your optimism. Each event, good or bad, is welcoming something better. Each action, whether successful or not is taking you to your next clue in attaining that outcome of which you may not be aware.

With a commitment to listening to your Inner Voice, you have agreed to take a journey on the ultimate amusement ride that delivers you only when the final doors open and you see the light.

That is the difference between those that need the reassurance of a ride taken once before and those that choose to listen to their Inner Voice, without regard to the fear or doubt of where it is taking them, and just strap on their seatbelts for an incredible ride.

A PRACTICE OF BEING

When you meditate, take note of the images or guidance you receive and consider if you accept this guidance willingly or choose to reject it. Are there messages that you receive that scare you or your mind takes over and moves you away from the guidance you receive? Take action on the guidance you receive, regardless of the fear or lack or practicality. See where it takes you.

Tears welled up in my eyes
as I begged for reassurance
that everything was going to be alright.
It was time.
A lifelong journey of finding my relationship with God
had come to a turning point.
'Was I really ready to listen to the voice
and act or
did I want to continue
the pattern of denying or rationalizing
the guidance I had received all these years.
Sure, I heard the voice in the past guide me
but it didn't make sense to me
or to be honest,
it just felt too uncomfortable
to follow the guidance of the voice within
that began speaking to me
almost 10 years ago.

Early 2002
From The Author's Journal
Personal Insights from a Meditation

PERSONAL INSIGHTS

TAKING BABY STEPS

We may be asked for the very first time in our life
to take actions
that may be contrary to our beliefs
or in contradiction to our rational mind.

A leap of faith. That is what taking baby steps is all about. When one recognizes the gifts that the Inner Voice brings, it can be scary to take those first steps toward implementing what we hear. Not only is it scary, it is like stepping out to the edge of the high dive and asking, "What the hell am I doing?" We may be asked for the very first time in our life to take actions that may be contrary to our beliefs or in contradiction to our rational mind. The rational mind frequently steps in and invalidates what we may have heard.

The challenging part, therefore, is really identifying what this voice sounds like. How can we be sure that it is what we really want it to be? Am I in tune with my Higher Self or am I a fake? After all, how can we expect to act on this Inner Voice when we really don't know when, and if, we hear it, right? How do we differentiate the difference between the Inner Voice and the ego speaking? It is too familiar to be redirected by the mind overriding the spirit within. The mind is such a powerful thing that turning it off in order to hear that voice that comes from within is challenging, to say the least. Confusing matters, how do we identify where this voice originates. Wouldn't it be easier to trust the voice if we could rely on its source, thereby giving credit where credit is due. But this Inner Voice continues to be elusive because it comes from a sense of inspiration; tell me where that comes from?

Given that people receive inspiration from a song, with a nature walk, or in an unexpected moment, how can you trust that the guidance you receive is the real deal. As we discussed in another chapter, many people experience the voice within in many different ways. Therefore, it is not imperative that we identify the origin or the authenticity of the Inner Voice; it is more important to develop a track record of listening and responding with sustainable results.

Too often we get caught up with the need to understand, to know. Why is it so important for us to have it so well defined and placed in a nice little package where we can place our faith? Much of what happens in our lives is not supported by sustainable evidence. If we fall in love, why fight it? If a great opportunity falls in our lap, why entrench ourselves with identifying the source or the evolution of the event? If we listen and act on what we hear and we are blessed with wonderful results, why question the definition of what it is?

I believe that it is crucial to develop a foundation for welcoming the voice within. Without a solid foundation, a house will crumble, a business will falter, a marriage will dissolve. With a foundation comes the basis from which you operate. This foundation has been discussed previously when I spoke of creating your space to listen, to be quiet and still, to establish a routine, and open up to the voice to appear when and where it comes. I have also shared the importance of not picking and choosing what you hear and what you act on. The voice within must be preserved in its integrity. Discarding or dismissing the truth about the messages from the Inner Voice is a common mistake many of us make because of many reasons, two of which are fear and the notion of failure.

Fear is felt and expressed in so many ways that it is difficult at times to identify it. Many of our negative thoughts can be attributed to our doubts, based on fear. Again, those things that have a greater importance to us are met with stronger feelings of fear. Because of our attachment to manifesting them in our lives, we attach fear as a mechanism to prevent the failure of successfully manifesting that which is so extremely important to us.

Fear can be seen as a lack of confidence. We lack confidence because we fear that we are not capable of accomplishing that which we seek. The notion of failure creates fear; without fear of failure there is a greater willingness to be. Because we have this notion that failure is bad, we fear the outcome of failure as bad and are therefore paralyzed and don't take action. If failure was not in your vocabulary and certainly not a concept that you understood, would you be more willing to try something. Most definitely.

If you were to look at failure as a blessing, an opportunity to celebrate learning and expanding as a human being, wouldn't you be more willing to take risks? What harm would there be if you took risk after risk after risk and never once put any energy on the idea you might fail...because failure doesn't exist. There would be no downside to taking risks because each of them would lead you to a better understanding, a better place in your life. Each setback is simply a lesson to grow and have more tools in your toolbox to make better choices in the future. So if you released fear and failure from your conceptual mind and willingly accepted that each and every experience you have in your life is for your good, wouldn't life be easier. Life would be grand. Self doubts would not exist, a lack of confidence would not be a deterring factor because, in the end, it doesn't really matter. There is no pain, no heartache, no disappointment. Experiences in life would be moving us towards that which we seek or simply redirecting us to where we truly need to be. There would be no disappointment or despair. It would simply be what is. That which is is that which is.

By opening our eyes to the opportunities that setbacks or "detours" bring us in our lives, we release one of the primary deterrents from acting on the powerful guidance of the voice within. We no longer need to pick and choose out of fear. We no longer need to avoid the nudges we get because they will lead us to where we need to go regardless of the outcome, regardless of our standards for success or self worth.

When we choose to step into guardianship of our own lives, it requires that we make goals or set our eyes on the life we want to live. I have spent years as a receptor of God's will and many months turned into years as I waited for the outcomes to drop at my feet. It doesn't work like that.

I spent several years developing a better understanding of the notion of surrender. In the beginning, I was challenged with the thought of letting go. That was way too foreign and uncomfortable for me. The thought of releasing it, by being out of control, and letting it unfold as it was destined to be was a concept beyond my ability to grasp. I let go of my need to be in control and waited. I waited for the miracles to come my way without my efforts. Isn't that what surrendering is all about. Letting go and letting God. God will just take care of it for me.

It reminds me of a story many of you have probably already heard before but I tell it because it illustrates this point so well. It is the story of the man caught in a flood. He prays for God to come and assist him and he lets it go. The waters reach the foundation of his house. A truck full of men appear and offer to take him to higher ground. "No, I'll be fine, thank you. God will rescue me." The water rises and fills his first floor. He moves to the second floor of his house. A boat passes by and he is called to, "Let us help you. Climb aboard." The man replies, "Thank you, no. It will all be taken care of by the will of God."

The waters continue to rise and the man is forced to the roof and a helicopter comes by and they throw him a rope, "grab on and we will pull you to safety." Again, he denies the help. He has surrendered to the situation and knows that God will rescue him. The man, having surrendered, yet planted in his conviction that God will miraculously come and rescue him, eventually drowns.

As the story goes, he enters heaven and catches a glimpse of God. Irritated, he storms up to God. "Where were you? I surrendered to your will and waited faithfully for you to come and rescue me. Nothing happened."

God, surprised, responds, "I don't understand. I sent you men in a truck, a boat was sent to your front door step, and a helicopter appeared in the sky above your head when the waters were reaching the top of your roof. Yet, not once, did you respond to me." Dumbfounded, the man replied, "Oh, that is what surrendering looks like." God questioned, "What did you think surrendering looked like?" The man thought for a while and admitted, "I don't really know. I just thought it would be more obvious, more miraculous." God reached out and touched the man on the shoulder and said, "Ordinary events turn into miracles when you act on them."

Our Higher Power doesn't deliver us the unimaginable; miracles are made available to us by connecting to our Source and allowing them to unfold in very ordinary (and unordinary) ways. While unexpected miracles do occur, it is more important that we recognize the ordinary ones that come to us in our daily lives. Simple ones. Ones that if we are not paying attention, we will miss them altogether. But they require a balance of guidance and self direction.

Coincidences and miracles do come along the way but they are "bonuses" to your efforts for acting on your own. I don't recall too many miracles coming to me during a time in my life that I thought God just did it all for me. I actually played a part. The willingness on my part to take the small steps and surrender to how they would lead me to where I needed to go. The presence of this "Understanding" was lacking in my life in many ways. Perhaps this absence was prevalent because I was absent. I was not engaged; I was not participating. I was expecting something far greater than what happened with the small baby steps I was taking in my life.

Try dancing with rhythm and grace with your partner absent of co-participation. So are the miracles of the Inner Voice. With the beauty and grace of this still voice comes a marriage of cooperation and trust. It is not enough to hear and then wait for the miracles to happen. Once you have heard the voice speak to you or events in your life happen or nudges guide you, you must take action. You must take the dance steps of life to match your partners moves, to be in synergy and "oneness" with the spirit.

When you begin your journey of listening to your Inner Voice, it is important that you begin by taking baby steps. It is a lot to ask that you dispel the notion of failure and fear and do so without falling back to old patterns or beliefs. Therefore, you need to strengthen these beliefs by reinforcing them with positive experiences that come from acting on the baby steps that are given to you by your Inner Voice. Don't expect to launch this courageous act of listening to your Inner Voice by changing your life in dramatic ways. Start first with the baby steps. Start with strengthening your confidence and the actualization of the accuracy of the voice within.

With each act of faith, you will not only build your confidence with your abilities to hear God's guidance and respond to the outreached Inner Voice in subtle and ordinary ways, but also you will build the confidence of the Inner Voice to raise the bar and push you to go farther, deeper, and more courageously.

A PRACTICE OF BEING

After meditating, write down all the images, ideas, notions, nudges, words, or thoughts that came to you. Go through the list, and cross out those things that you know, for a fact, came from your mind, like tasks to complete or duties to perform that you believe were ego-driven or manipulated by your mind. Now, focus on those remaining on the paper. Pick one that you might have some resistance to, a small baby step, and commit to acting on it. See what happens.

I got a strong message over the weekend
while I was meditating
to call someone.
So, acting on the inner voice, I did.
It was someone that I hadn't seen or talked to in a long time.
I admitted I had this strong urge to call her, so I did.
We chatted. It was nice.
We exchanged addresses.
I hung up and felt great that I acted on my 'inner voice'.
I did not know where it was going to take me
but that was okay.
It was the act of doing so.

December 11, 2001
From The Author's Journal
Personal Insights from a Meditation

PERSONAL INSIGHTS

PERSONAL INSIGHTS

FAITH & COURAGE

When it makes no sense,
you do it anyway.

If there is one thing that I have learned about listening to the Inner Voice it is that it requires an inordinate amount of faith and courage. I'm not talking about the type of faith we have come to understand. That faith is believing in a Higher Power that will deliver us a good life. I'm talking about having faith with ourselves. This faith is not about a belief that is out there, elusive and immeasurable.

This is a belief, a knowing, an acceptance of what is real, what is measurable. It is a belief, a faith that we are special enough to hear the Inner Voice. It is a faith, a conviction, that each and every one of us is blessed with this ability in the same way we are blessed with the miracle of breath.

While we take for granted our ability to take air in and out as routinely as the passing of the day, our faith in our innate ability to listen to the Inner Voice is necessary in order that we might accept this skill, this talent, as ordinary and routine. It gives us the permission to act on what we hear. And faith is what it takes to hold off the nay sayers and the disbelievers when it comes to taking the steps in honoring the guidance of the Inner

Voice. It requires courage to stay the course and know deep down in your heart that the unconventional measures you might be undertaking are the right ones.

Courage is necessary to take the Inner Voice at its word and step in fully when all other indicators say otherwise. It is in this courage and faith that we are truly tested with our devotion to the Inner Voice. When it presents itself, we are enriched and rewarded like no other time with miracles and blessings far beyond measure. It requires more of us to respond to the Inner Voice than to reject it. It requires more of us to accept that each and every one of us has the ability to hear that Inner Voice. That, however, is the easy part. Acting on it is the challenging, trying part. It takes little courage and faith to tap into that quiet voice within. All that is required is patience and perseverance. The big shift is trusting the Inner Voice and acting on it when all conventions dictate otherwise.

If each person would take twenty minutes each and every day and sit in silence, they would ultimately hear the Inner Voice. Routine offers that gift graciously. The greatness in a person is when they possess the courage and the strength to take steps that may be questioned by others, follow guidance that is unproven, and ride the waves of insights, however brilliant or still they may be. When one is stretched to his or her limits of rational thinking, when one is on the edge of the absurd, when one has fallen out of acceptable norms of behavior, that is when the faith and courage is tested. It takes courage and faith to stay the course when not only your friends and family members are questioning you but you are questioning yourself.

I wouldn't say I have been a very practical person. Most people would not refer to me as conventional. And yet when I committed to following the guidance I received from the Inner Voice, I was put to the test. That is when it became clear to me that you can't pick and choose what you hear and what you act on. If you really want the guidance of the Inner Voice, you have to respect it by following what guidance you receive. That is where you develop your faith and your courage. It takes a lot to act on blind faith.

Much of what you will hear from your Inner Voice you know at some level that it is true but it scares the heck out of you. I have, without a doubt, taken a position that, if asked, 99 out of 100 people would consider my actions as highly irresponsible when it comes to the management of money during these times of trusting the Inner Voice. When most people would suggest that I just go get a job to pay the bills, I stayed the course. When I asked for direction from my Inner Voice, it said, *"Stay the course."*

When I asked how I might survive these challenging financial times, the Inner Voice said, *"Finish your book."* I know enough that the process of finishing the writing is just the beginning. After that is the editing, the cover design, finding the publisher, printing the book, marketing the book and then selling the book. That is certainly not an immediate fix to my need for income right now. I have found that when I am in a moment of financial need, somehow, I am provided for. I trust that my guidance to *"finish the book"* and to honor it by acting on it will deliver me where I need to go—even if that means letting go of all that I own on this material plane of existence.

But the simple truth is that I have committed myself to listening and responding each day, each week with the guidance I receive. I am either right on the mark or I have lost my mind.

Either way, isn't that what we are trying to do—"lose our mind"? (I now look at this phrase with a new perspective. Losing our mind is a good thing!) Nevertheless, I will not know until some uncertain time in the future. That is the risk. That is the faith. That is the courage. It is far easier to not listen than to trust the unknown.

For nearly two years, I lived on blind faith that the steps I was taking and the guidance I was listening to was true and accurate. Accurate, because I was living in the moment and following what I was directed to do at the time. Repeatedly, again and again, my Inner Voice said, "*Complete the book.*" For over twenty years I didn't write a book because I'd heard stories of defeated writers—that you can't make any money at it; I thought I had to be special to write about something as awesome as our Inner Voice. I didn't see a book as the end all and be all in creating financial abundance or any kind of financial security.

Initially, I intended to write an entirely different book. A book about parenting. But I listened. And this time, I dutifully sat down and began without even knowing what it was going to be. I let go of the attachment to the impact it might make and just took the first baby step, one right after another. Soon I had several chapters. It doesn't make sense; ironically when I needed the money more than ever, I spent valuable time during the workday writing my book.

That is the courage and faith I am talking about. When it makes no sense, you do it anyway. And now I reflect and my rational mind says, "Well, Mark, now that you are writing the book, how do you know if it was the best use of your precious time?" And my answer, "I don't know but I do know that the process was the right thing to do at the time; it will take me to where I am supposed to be, regardless of the success or profitability from the book." With bills mounting, I go to my chair to meditate. Month after month I have gone deeper and deeper into debt. I frequently awake in the middle of the night alarmed, scared, fearful and full of doubt because my mind takes over. It takes me hours to get back to sleep. I find my nights to be my worst. While sleeping, my mind congers up all reasons for despair and hopelessness. The negative thoughts are overwhelming at times. I want to give in; I want to return to the old way of living my life with more security, sensibility. Everything possible collapses during those dreadful nights of doubt. Half asleep, in a dreamlike state, my faith and courage doesn't have a fighting chance.

I often climb into my meditation chair at three o'clock in the morning because I feel guided to do so. Although I might be exhausted, and the motivation to pull myself out of bed is lacking, I do it because I am called to do so. Not doing so would suggest that I don't believe in the power of my natural knowing, my Inner Voice calling me to "listen." I sit in the darkness and take several deep breaths and ask that I be given a wakeup call. "Tell me what to do. Tell me if I am being crazy. I feel I'm being crazy. Do I activate my real estate license? Do I take on a job at Home Depot or Costco? Please direct me so that I can serve my highest good." And the voice repeatedly says, "*Go write the book; just finish the book.*"

For each early morning that I have received this reassuring voice, I can count dozens and dozens of times I have had the exact same experience, "*Write the book.*" How can I deny that? How can I negate that directive and go get a $10-per-hour job because it is considered the right thing to do, the responsible thing to do? Each time that I turned within, the message was consistent. There was never a, "Mark, it is time to be responsible now. You need to go get a job to pay the bills and pay for your children's college education, etc., etc." None of that. There was never a time that the voice directed me to do any thing other than, "*Write the book,*" so I'm writing the book! I can't explain it. I have asked my family to not try to understand it; I struggle with understanding it myself. This is the Courage and Faith I speak of. Beyond all reasoning, follow the guidance of the Inner Voice.

Not to belabor the point, the Inner Voice is not guided by reason but by a knowing that we can never come to fully understand; the Inner Voice is solely directed to guide us toward our highest purpose in that exact period of time.

That is why I believe that the voice did direct me to write the book and I do surrender to the outcome; if it should be an unsuccessful endeavor, I know that writing the book will take me to where I need to go. It is in my willingness to trust in the moment that I can let go of my attachment to what I perceive the outcome will be. Why? Because the voice told me so. It is that simple: Faith and Courage to follow my Inner Voice.

A PRACTICE OF BEING

After you meditate or receive some inspiration you consider your Higher Power speaking to you, take the first small baby step of action. Then stop. Take notice. What are you experiencing? What new opportunities have you come upon? Look around. What do you notice? Is there anything that appears to be a coincidence? If so, act on it. Follow the nudges. Consider yourself on your own treasure hunt. Follow the clues. Where does it take you in the end? Is there an end? A pause? A continuation later in time?

I can no longer
ignore the voice that says, 'Go write.'
In the best of times and in the worst of times,

The voice says, 'Write.'
It's hard to believe that this is the right thing to do
Under the circumstances.
It makes no sense.

December 6, 2001
From The Author's Journal
Personal Insights from a Meditation

PERSONAL INSIGHTS

IT'S EASIER TO NOT LISTEN

My life was simpler
when I didn't need to consider
what the Inner Voice thought
or if it was real, or if it was accurate.

At the age of 21, I was introduced to the world of personal growth workshops. I dug in right away. I ate it up. I loved the pops of awareness, the social thing, the inspiration from the front-of-the-room-gurus, and how it dramatically changed my life forever. I went from a pretty conservative, traditional way of thinking to a whole new way of understanding of how life really presents itself. I left behind the black and white thinking and jumped into the world of shades of white. Not gray but shades of positive thinking. A world where the glass is half full and the experiences we have are a reflection of our thinking, the hidden beliefs we hold, and the lessons we need to learn. I entered an era when people were questioning the consciousness movement and what it meant to be "aware." The young man from Portland, Oregon, raised in a family principled by acceptable norms of behavior, expanded and transformed into a free thinker that saw the possibilities rather than the obstacles. I was forever changed.

Shortly after my first workshop, I recall talking with a friend about my new-found philosophy. "It is so much more challenging to think this way, but I could never go back to the way I used to think." Since then, I have heard countless number of people experiencing the same expansion of their thinking and the evolution of their awareness say the same thing. In my coaching with parents, I share with them that it is far easier to say, "No," than to put in the effort to understand your teenager and come to a mutual agreement.

The same holds true when it comes to listening to our Inner Voice. It is easier to not listen. Listening requires effort. Listening requires a willingness to accept that which might be different from how we saw it in the past. Listening requires us to be open to the unknown, the unfamiliar. Listening requires discipline, while failure to turn within requires no effort at all. But once you listen, once you hear that quiet voice within deliver a pearl of wisdom, it is difficult to go back to the old way of doing things.

I have had several false starts when it came to listening. Too many to count. I would try every way possible to meditate so that I could hear that voice that others talked about. Nothing happened. My mind raced. I thought about the tasks I should be doing instead of attempting to meditate.

I became frustrated because I wasn't doing it right. I beat myself up because I didn't have what it takes. Back to back days of meditating turned into once a week, turned into once a month, turned into "I forgot the last time I meditated." It was just too frustrating to work so hard at it and have nothing come of it. Expectations were high, I admit. However, hearing nothing after years got old, real fast. It was easy to blow it off when my life was working well. It was easy to rationalize that I didn't have what it takes. It was easy to fill that time with productive tasks that disguised my intuitive nature with an increase in notable and measurable outcomes. Why meditate when I can accomplish so much without? It became my mantra to do rather than be. Doing brought me greater satisfaction. If meditating is Being then I wasn't very impressed.

But in my lowest moments, I would always return to my efforts to hear the voice, to receive the guidance I needed during those times of crisis. Repeatedly my desperation turned into discipline and I found myself once again searching for reassurance from the quiet voice within. "Why," I asked myself, "do I always return to my desire to tap that inner resource?" I desired guidance and validation. I wanted to be hopeful that I could, some day, be blessed with the ability to tap that inner resource I believed was there, but hidden from me.

Of course, during difficult times, people turn to prayer and religion for solace. I cannot deny that I too turned to that search within when I was in a time of need. But why did I go inside? Why did I not drop to my knees and look to the skies? I returned to the quiet place and looked within. Something told me that is where I needed to go. Finally it came. I was not ignored. I was not disappointed. Not only did I hear the voice and recognized it as real, it tested me by directing me to go write about the power of intuition, the ability to listen to the voice within.

Wait a moment! I search for the skills of tapping my intuition, the power of my natural knowing and it calls me to go write about it. "Who am I?" I asked. I am certainly not the expert. I don't have those special skills I have witnessed with the spiritual teachers with which I have come into contact. So why am I being asked to write about this rare or unusual talent? Looking back, I realize now that this calling was the beginning of a whole new adventure for me; my awakening. To get the message, it had to be big. With this new direction, it dispelled the notion of having to be perfect at it, to do it a certain way, to understand that everyone has the gift, the power to tap into their natural knowing.

I began to write and with each day, it began to flow easier and easier until I realized I was out of my body as I wrote the words that came to the page. I began to carry on a conversation with myself, by myself. I would ask the question and let it go. I placed my fingers on the keyboard and began to type the first word that came to mind, never knowing what the final sentence would be. I trusted that it would come. I trusted that it came in pieces, one segment at a time. I let go of trying to figure out what I was going to say. It didn't matter. I just wrote and wrote and wrote.

And as I expanded my faith so did the power of my Inner Voice. Over time, I came to hear the voice more readily, almost routinely. It felt natural, not forced or manufactured. For me, my Inner Voice commanded me to write about the significance of this awakening in such a powerful way, how could I deny it? Over time, my writing became more prolific. I expanded my trust and faith. Although I was hesitant to share my experience with anyone, I finally told my mother about the writing exercises I was doing. She was both intrigued and curious. Curious about the validity of this exercise.

By testing my concepts, she caused me to question my authenticity and I began to pick away at my journal and challenge the comments made by my Inner Voice until one day my doubt was so high, my skepticism so great, I closed my laptop and didn't return for nearly two years. It was far easier for me to just not listen. To move on with my life without the pretenses that what I was hearing was legitimate.

I returned to a world that didn't require me to be responsible for my beliefs or what may have been perceived as my ego-driven desire to be special and uniquely qualified as a spiritual teacher. That responsibility was far too great for me. The whole time I was writing, I was fighting it and denying it. It caused me grief and disappointment. I just couldn't get past this idea that I wasn't qualified, that I didn't really have this unique talent to tap into my inner self.

I challenged myself all along the way. "Who am I?" I asked repeatedly. Who am I to think I am special enough to have this experience? It was easier to turn away than to face these plaguing questions. It was much easier to move along with my life, living outside the box rather than within. It was far easier to make my decisions and live my life without the pressure and responsibility of doing it with the guidance of my Inner Voice. It was far less stressful to not have to wonder if I was a fake—if my ego was running away with me.

I discovered I could live a very productive, peaceful life if I elected not to test myself, not to listen to the power of my intuitive voice, my natural knowing, my Inner Voice—whatever you want to call it. My life was simpler when I didn't need to consider what the Inner Voice thought or if it was real or if it was accurate. I stepped away from my meditation and I closed the door to my desire to trust my Inner Voice.

Years went by and during that time I went through a stressful divorce and experienced pain like I had never felt before. My 18-year marriage behind me and my life ahead of me, I didn't know what I really wanted to do with my life. I began meeting with a spiritual life coach and we began the process of asking, "now what?" After several meetings, it became clear that I really wanted to be a public speaker and share my experiences with those going through tough times. I saw myself speaking at churches and before audiences hungry for the skills to tap into their natural knowing. It was all coming back to me now. It made perfect sense. I dug deeper and deeper and realized there was a reason I kept my tattered director's chair all those years. I finally determined what my life's work was. Absolutely. It was my destiny.

Then, months later, without warning, I walked into my coaching session and declared that wasn't it and I was going to pursue my real estate business. I'm sure I threw him completely off guard and he undoubtedly thought I had lost my mind. Regardless, this was the journey I felt I had to take. I have to laugh when I look back at those days. Once again, I denounced my authentic journey because of fear. I feared that I wouldn't be able to make enough money, be good enough, credible enough, to support myself so I retracted to what I knew, real estate. That was safe, that was automatic. But there was something different this time. This time I committed to listening to the Inner Voice regardless of the impracticality or the rationality of the decisions I made. I vowed to listen and react to the voice within. And I did exactly that and continue to do so today.

I don't know if my life would be that much different now if I had acted on my desire to do public speaking. Time will only tell. Perhaps the change to real estate was a necessary detour to get me to where I needed to be. I do know that the path that I took was necessary for my journey to embrace my Inner Voice completely in its entirety. I never wavered on what the voice told me. When I asked for direction, it routinely encouraged me to continue with my endeavors. That course took me to the bottom where I lost my home and finally awoke to who I really am. I can't recall a time when I was more at peace and happy with the uncertainty of my unfolding life. For all those years in the past, I had this image of who I was and lost the truth about what it is to truly respond to your Inner Voice. I looked to be validated by the work I did in real estate only to find that when I lost it all, I came home to who I really wanted to be and the Inner Voice took me there. I learned that the Inner Voice doesn't always deliver bliss and certainty.

My Inner Voice took me on a necessary detour that opened my eyes and lifted my doubt so that I could finally accept that the only way to live is to listen to the Inner Voice. Even though it took me to some very low points in my life, I realize now, more than ever, that I can't go back to the old way of living my life. It is far more rewarding and easier to listen to the voice within and trust that my authentic journey will take me to my perfect destination.

A PRACTICE OF BEING

After meditating several times and you receive similar guidance that has alarmed you in the past, respond to the guidance by taking action, regardless of the fear, and see what happens.

*Even though I would bet my life
those words were spoken to me,
do you think I embraced them
and made their meaning a practice in my life.
No way.
That meant giving up too much.
I relished in the idea I had heard them
but I wasn't quite ready to make them real for me.
I had still too much at stake.
Interestingly, these words came at a time when I had it all.
I ignored the advice.*

November 5, 2001
From The Author's Journal
Personal Insights from a Meditation

PERSONAL INSIGHTS

PERSONAL INSIGHTS

DON'T TRY TO UNDERSTAND

*The Inner Voice truly works in the moment
and reflects its guidance to where we are at that given time
or what we need to hear in that moment.*

Plugging your nose and jumping in. That is just about
what it takes to strengthen the power of the voice within. For
years I would meditate and then pull forth that which made
sense and ignore that which didn't. I just couldn't understand
why the Inner Voice would direct me in a certain way. Much of
what I heard went against convention. What was reasonable and
acceptable was pushed to the limits. What I have come to learn
is that it is not about understanding why the voice speaks in the
way it does. What is important is listening and accepting it with
blind faith and acting on it. That is why taking Baby Steps is so
important. You need to build your confidence with the Inner
Voice by taking small steps that dispels much of your fear and
trepidation. When we let go of the need to understand and act
on what we hear, we are rewarded with an Inner Voice that is
more vocal. We cannot pick and choose what we hear.

In the beginning of your faith with the Inner Voice, don't
be surprised if you choose to challenge it. After all, you may be
questioning where this voice comes from, if it is legitimate, and if
what it shares is reasonable. We are naturally suspicious people

and therefore we question that which we can't substantiate. And the Inner Voice cannot be substantiated. All we can do is continue to look inside and trust that the voice is there.

We can act on the guidance we receive and determine for ourselves if we are believers. But along the way, we might question the validity. "Who are we to hear this voice within?" I know that I repeatedly challenged the voice. I tested it. I asked for guidance on one day and then asked for the same guidance on the next, only to find different responses.

I recall one experience where I exclaimed, "You are a fake." I had progressed fairly well with my discipline of listening to the voice within. I had developed a routine and a strong belief that the voice was legitimate and real. I relied on it for guidance. I trusted the words and put the guidance into play in my life. All was going well until I found the guidance offered varied responses that caused me to doubt and discard my practice. I asked a question one day, and then again the next day, and got different answers. How could this be? I lost confidence and faith in the Inner Voice.

I put away my "stream of consciousness" writing. I lost faith with my Spiritual Intelligence. I stopped meditating. I was too frustrated. I lost hope. I reluctantly accepted that I only hoped that I had the abilities to hear this sacred voice from within. I now questioned whether it was possible at all. Months turned into nearly two years. I did little to call upon my once trusted friend. The voice went dormant.

Years later, one evening I was cleaning up my laptop when I came across my journal that recorded the guidance I had received from my Inner Voice. At the top of the document read,

"Are You Talking to Me?" Ninety-seven pages followed. I had forgotten I had written so much. My curiosity renewed, I began to read. I recalled I had learned to type the words that came to me in the moment without regard to the sentence structure or what I wanted to say. I trusted the first word that came to me and the balance of the sentenced just followed. I suspended traditional forms of education that suggested you formulate an outline of what you wanted to say and then build from there. I just simply sat down and wrote. I would ask a question and then sit in silence until I was moved to type, never knowing what I was going to say.

As I revisited this practice, I came across this entry:

"It all begins with us as the source. I am the source. I am where the beginning starts. I am the head of the stream, the source of the flow. It all begins with me. I am the source for the choices I make and the decisions that I choose. I am the source from which it all begins.

Knowing this enables me to open the gates and allow the flow, the source, to take its course.

Repeating I am the Source does magical things; it frees the mind and opens the spirit, the Inner Voice, the Higher Power to speak.

Taking ownership that it all begins with you discards the notions that outside sources effect and direct us.

In truth, we are the Source and it is in acknowledging it and honoring it that the Source becomes stronger, more confident and clear. By acting on the simple things that the Source suggests opens up a world much greater and more powerful. I am the SOURCE. When you hear, 'consider the source', know now that the power of that statement lies within."

Hello? What more did I need to know? It was time. It was beyond a reasonable time. I again surrendered to the process and let go of my need to be in control of what I was going to say. To judge it. To question it.

Once again, I was amazed at what fell upon these written pages. When I determined I was a fake and concluded all of this was manufactured in my mind and in my desire to feel special and gifted, I stopped with my writing and let it go like it was a bad experience I didn't want to recall ever again.

My anger and frustration were my last thoughts on the pages of these journal entries. It was clear from my review that I was frustrated to such a degree that I abandoned any sense of closure. I had stopped midstream. All of this was a fabrication of my ego. Or, at least, that is what I thought when I ended my journaling over six years ago.

Now, years later, I revisited my "journal of spiritual intelligence" and to my surprise I discovered a very different experience. I shared this writing style with only my mother. Even then, I was reluctant because it seemed so whacky, even to me. However, I read about things that had actually happened since I made the entry. Several things I had written years before were written with precision and accuracy. Many of them had come true. I realized that my interpretation of what I was writing was strongly influenced by my conscious mind passing judgment. I took what I had written from the essence of my inner knowing and critiqued it by my rational mind that needed to understand and make sense of it.

The truth, I learned, in reflecting back is that the Inner Voice doesn't require the same degree of validation. The Inner

Voice simply speaks what comes and that is only the truth in that moment. I saw a pattern that showed with "routine meditation" a stream of consciousness that made sense. Taking it out of context and interpreting only a segment of the message would surely suggest errors and falsehoods, if reviewed by the rational mind.

When I tried to understand or interpret with rational reasoning, I found it would often suggest that the words were false or contradictory. When I went back to earlier entries and followed the path of dialogue, I found that the very contradictions that forced me to abandon my beliefs were attempts at that time to combat doubts by "testing" the Inner Voice. I noticed I would ask the same question over and over again, day after day, and get a different answer. I believe that since I was so engaged with the Inner Voice that it was not able to detect my challenges and answer my "trick questions" with brutal honesty in that moment.

I also concluded that the Inner Voice truly works in the moment and reflects its guidance to where we are at that given time or what we need to hear in that moment. It might be similar to being blunt with someone about a sensitive issue or choosing to break it to them slowly.

In the end the message is the same. I found references from my journaling that suggested the voice was inquiring in ways to set me straight. I found entries like, "*I thought you were…*" or "*Isn't that what you wanted all along?*" to "*If this is what you have been asking for then why must you resist?*" I was so disappointed to learn that I had abandoned my journaling and my mediation all those years ago because I allowed my rational mind to pass judgment on my Inner Voice.

While I was initially discouraged for the loss of valuable time, I discovered that many of the comments made by the Inner Voice were accurate, especially the guidance to teach the words of my mother, Karma. I had taken the guidance and began interviewing her because my practical mind translated it that way.

When it didn't work well, I passed judgment on the accuracy of the Inner Voice. Now years later, without referring back to my journal, I have launched a non-profit foundation in honor of my mother that "expresses her philosophy and the essence of the work I am doing" not her specific words.

I failed to listen. I failed to act. I tried to understand, justify, rationalize and interpret the Inner Voice so it fit into my level of conscious thinking. A big lesson learned.

Now, I listen and release my need to understand or question the truth in it. I have learned it is unimportant. The voice speaks in baby steps and I just need to put one foot forward and trust like I did with my fingers on the keyboard.

THE PRACTICE OF BEING

Meditate. Without thinking, rationalizing, processing, justifying or trying to bring reason to what you hear, act on it. See what happens.

Pushy, pushy, pushy.
You always want specific steps.
The unknown is very uncomfortable for you.
You need to know each step at a time.
The sooner you become more comfortable with taking a step
without knowing exactly what is going to happen
or where it is going to lead you,
the further you will go and
the more you will accomplish.

Why is it that you have this need
To Understand?
Can you explain everything in life?
Of course not.
But for some reason it is necessary for man to need to explain
his thinking, his feelings, his life's goals and passions
and why he does or did something.
It is not enough for it to just be.

April 16-24, 2003
From The Author's Journal
Inner Voice Speaking

PERSONAL INSIGHTS

THERE ARE NO GUARANTEES
WITH LISTENING

By listening,
one should prepare for a larger void,
an understanding that has no limits or practicality.

I had this belief that if you were able to tap into your Inner Voice you would be able to receive guidance that would lead you to your perfect world. I believed that having this ability to listen and hear your Inner Voice would guide you in the most intricate parts of your life and you would be blessed with ease and simplicity. I held onto the notion that the power of the quiet, still voice was capable of freeing me from conflicts and disappointments.

Over time, that belief has changed dramatically. I have come to believe that there are no guarantees with listening. I have learned that listening and acting on the guidance given by our natural knowing isn't enough to assure us perfect living. Quite the contrary, responding to your Inner Voice will challenge you in ways you never thought possible. Your commitment to listening will open doors that cause you to act in ways once considered unreasonable. Your need for understanding will diminish and your faith in the unknown will become stronger. You will not be able to explain your actions, merely blindly accept them and step forward with conviction. This blind faith is what makes the power of the Inner Voice immeasurable to anything you have experienced in the past. I think that is what makes a commitment to listening to the Inner Voice so profound.

With the desire to listen, we move more fully in preparing ourselves for our future. By listening, one should prepare for a larger void, an understanding that has no limits or practicality. Stepping into the call for inner guidance, there is also a call to accept that which is delivered, despite unnatural or unpredictable events.

One must surrender to the need to know. Step by step, moment by moment, your life will unfold without reason at times and without a clear direction most of the time. All the while, there remains a peace and certainty of action. A knowingness falls over you and you are willing to embark on journeys never before considered. This willingness is the confidence that comes with being validated by the accuracy of the Inner Voice. When you reach that place that you accept all as perfect and accurate in your life, then you begin to accept all events, both positive and negative, as perfect expressions of the hidden treasure that lies within our secret vault.

You might welcome a setback as an opportunity to see things differently or take you in a direction you hadn't considered in the past. Obstacles become opportunities. Disasters become blessings in disguise.

Because of your new way of looking at things, a greater peace comes over you because you no longer fear disappointments. If negative events in your life are not met with grief and despair but rather with hope of change and a better tomorrow, there will be less worry about your outcome. It is all a part of the plan. With the good, comes the bad. With the downturn, comes the lesson. With the detour, comes the awakening.

The only guarantee is that you will be delivered. Staying true to the Inner Voice will land you where you need to be. Some arrive unscathed while others are less fortunate. Who is to say why? Some may attribute it to past Karma. Others might suggest that they were less aware and stumbled into more lessons for learning. I might suggest that we create the exact experiences we need to attract in our lives so that we might better accept the truth of the Inner Voice.

My school of hard knocks have taken me closer to peace and my passion and purpose. For whatever reason, it was not enough for me to learn from positive experiences; I had to experience the pain so I could taste the joy. I was dumber than I look because it took me so long to learn the simple truths about the Inner Voice. That truth being that all people have the ability to call upon their Inner Voice. It is not a scary thing or a thing that requires a high degree of responsibility. It is as simple as breathing air and taking your next step along the path. Complicating the existence of the Inner Voice only hampers its true expression and leaves you with discontent.

Open up to the nudge from within- the sooner the better. Leave behind the doubt and burden you may think it represents. Open to the possibilities that each and everyone of us can simply and easily access God's presence by accepting first that we can. Accepting the oxygen we breath is as simple as accepting the awakening soul within.

With each breath of acceptance comes an ease. With ease comes acceptance. The cycle continues and in time they become one. It becomes quite easy to accept that that nudge is real and acting on it is no more difficult than reciting the alphabet or the blink of an eye or an extension of a hand shake.

We take that all for granted and yet we challenge ourselves with the acceptance of our ability to seek truth by going within. As a matter of routine, the act of calling forth that Inner Voice strengthens it's presence not only during meditation but in our daily living. Once a daily ritual, it matters not whether the voice speaks of purpose and rightful direction or sends us into a whirling downward spiral that teaches us far greater lessons than those we would have noticed along the path of simplicity.

We begin to ask not the favor of our outcomes but welcome the moment by moment brilliance of the small steps we take. It matters not if it takes us down our intended path because we will certainly return to our place of belonging with greater conviction. We let go of the concept of failure because it means nothing to us. Instead we celebrate by embracing all matters of physical expression as perfect. There is neither good nor bad. It is only what it is. And what it is is simply an expression of our inner compass that, in this moment, is directing us down a certain path.

It makes no difference if it takes us longer, if we see more pitfalls, if we enjoy more distractions. It is what it is and that is the beauty of listening to the Inner Voice without questioning each little baby step along the way. With the unyielding faith that comes from the validation of feeling in sync with our destiny, we are at peace with knowing that there is no wrongful direction.

THE PRACTICE OF BEING

Take an example of a choice you made in your life that took you down the wrong road, or, at least, you thought so. Regardless, it brought you pain and suffering. In the end, how was it all perfect for you? What did you learn or how did you grow that you might not have if you had not experienced this setback? Trust your guidance with blind faith. Accept where you are is perfect.

Do you realize that the pain and suffering
that you have had has been
the fuel to move you closer to your dreams?
Moving you closer to actualizing
to that what you really want.
Easy and comfortable
has not moved you.
You needed to create suffering
so that you would do something about it.
To get committed enough,
to get down and get into it.
Part of the pain
was for your personal growth
and understanding
and part of it,
largely,
was a motivator
to get you to take action.

April 16, 2003
From The Author's Journal
Inner Voice Speaking

PERSONAL INSIGHTS

BE OPEN TO DETOURS

That is the miracle of relinquishing your plans
and allowing the miracles of detours
to come your way.

I've had my fair share of detours in my life. I'm a goal setter; I make a plan and work the plan. And despite all this, my life has been blessed with many detours. Detours as most people might refer to as setbacks. For me, these setbacks have become great learning opportunities. They have introduced me to things and to experiences that I would not have considered putting on my "bucket list."

I have come to enjoy, to appreciate, my detours. They were initially upsetting and problematic but now I welcome them as a matter of routine. It is all about letting go of the attachments in our lives. When we are so fixed on the outcome, we fail to see the obvious opportunities that come along the way. When I recall the blessings that I have had in my life, many of them are attributed to detours. The path that I was taking, the direction I was going, the plan that I was working got interrupted by some circumstance that took me down another road and pleasantly introduced me to a more favorable outcome. Not necessarily that the outcome was favorable but what I derived from my experience was favorable. Many of my detours have been real learning lessons. They were painful and frustrating. Often times I would fight them and resist them. Why? It was not the course I was planning on taking. I wanted to be in control of my destiny. I wanted to know what was happening next and then what came after that. I made specific plans and they were thwarted by some event that took me completely off my course. Or did it? Perhaps the detour was exactly the course I was intended to take.

I love that my 18 year old daughter, Taylor, has already got this one figured out. She always says, "Well, things will always turn out the way they are supposed to." She has learned at an early age to accept the course. To welcome what it brings. She doesn't wait and see. She acts, and then reflects, and then acts, and then awaits her destiny.

This series of new ideas redirects you down a path that ultimately makes more sense. Call it fate. Call it divine intervention. It does not matter. What matters is that you don't resist it. Fighting the detour will only prolong your journey or enhance the lesson learned.

Detours can come without drama or they can come with great strain and turbulence. The choice is up to us. After all, perhaps the detour is more likely to be the direct route than the direct route itself. Is it Divine intervention that redirects you toward your purposeful route or away from it? Knowing that it is all perfect, either way, you are a winner. Take the ticket for the ride. You are assured it will be well worth it.

Coincidental detours merely happen. You might be heading down the sidewalk and something catches your eye in a storefront. You stop for a moment to look, then you continue on with a hurried pace. You think you might be late for your appointment so you take an uncharted shortcut through the lobby of a building. For some reason you were moved to take a different course, turning the corner, you exit the lobby and you bump into a friend you haven't seen for quite some time. That reunion leads to a fabulous outcome and you find yourself amazed that it happened so coincidentally. Or did it? Was it the Universal Energy working its magic to bring the two of you together?

The key is going with the flow. Other detours may not be as positive. They may be devastating. Like the loss of my dream home, they may take you where you really don't want to go. But there is a lesson there. The key is you don't fight it. You had this nudge to try something different or you tried something with all the confidence in the world and it didn't work out. You have to face the reality you have to go in a different direction. As with my house, don't always expect miracles to happen every time you take a detour but expect that they can happen if you let them. Be open. Be receptive.

When you find yourself in a detour in life, be responsive to the events that happen as a result. Don't discard happenings as accidental or insignificant. A new person met, a reconnection, a new business discovered, a contact made, a painful lesson learned. They are all perfectly significant. And possibly, just possibly, there isn't a significant experience this time. Perhaps this new found detour will bring you results at a later time when the miracle does happen.

Several years ago, I was heavily entrenched in my career as a real estate sales agent. We had a gentleman come to the office to give demonstrations of website templates his company had developed. I was running errands that morning and had no intention of going into the office, let alone sit through a sales presentation on real estate websites. I was more interested in getting out of real estate at the time.

Well, I had a nudge to drop by the office and check my mail. I was not expecting any important letters, and I did not make special trips into the office just to check my mail. This day was different. So I ran in for a quick stop, only to run right into the middle of the demonstration. Realizing that it was our typical Monday morning meeting, I pulled up a chair and sat down as if I had intended on attending the presentation. Within minutes, I was engulfed with the possibilities of what the website could do for me professionally. Not real estate. But for my speaking and coaching business that laid dormant in the far recesses of my mind.

After everyone left, I stayed and talked with him and learned what this website search engine optimization stuff could do to drive people to my site. The mere idea of it re-enthused me to such an excitement, I went right to my computer and began googling "public speaker", "trainer", "facilitator" and to my surprise up popped an advertisement for a trainer and public speaker to work at a company in San Juan Capistrano in Southern California.

I will never forget the moment I searched for their website and found that their offices overlooked the Pacific Ocean. Could this be for real? I had always wanted to move to Southern California for the sun and now I found the opportunity to do so with a company that suited my career goals to the tee. I applied for the job, was hired and relocated to Dana Point, California and began a new career that has served me beyond measure. If I had not responded to that nudge to go to the office, if I had not responded to the presentation, had I not searched the net, I would not have found my dream job. The idea of it would never have even entered my mind.

My detour that day changed my life. It was not in the game plan for me to relocate to Southern California. That morning, I did not wake up and say, "I'm going to quit my job in real estate and become a personal growth trainer for a company in Southern California." That is the miracle of relinquishing your plans and allowing the miracles of detours to come your way.

The detours that aren't so pleasant are the more difficult ones to get the blessings from. I call these the "hit the brick wall" detours. Under no circumstances are you able to continue with your original plan. A detour is imminent. Sometimes with warning, sometimes without warning. What makes these detours so challenging is that we usually have a vested interest in the outcome. There is a significant attachment to the results and therefore a significant resistance to it failing. When we don't get what we want, we consider it a failure, a lack of.

Letting go and accepting it for what it is can be very challenging. At some level, I think we bring on these failures as big lessons for us to consider alternatives plans. Some have great intentions and well thought out plans and they still meet with road blocks. With the best of intentions, we fall flat on our face and we must look at it objectively and decide we must move on. What do they say, "doing the same thing over and over and expecting the same outcome is a definition of insanity." So these great goals, the great plans we scheme up in our minds and we put to action are sometimes for a bigger lesson learned: meeting with resistance, letting go, and moving in another direction. We are simply setting up the opportunity for us to see a better outcome via a self-emposed detour.

Obviously unconsciously, we set ourselves up to experience setbacks so we can look at things differently. We give ourselves permission to learn a valuable lesson when we don't listen to the Inner Voice and act in ways that are certain to give us hard earned detours. I'm not saying that we always set ourselves up to crash and burn. However, if we were to look at the choices we made, a good percentage of the time, we can recognize the inherent obstacles, barriers or shortfalls that we ignored. Lost in our ego or our zest for "taking the easier road" we placed our self in harms way by setting ourselves up with failure and thereby invaluable life lessons.

Don't get me wrong, I believe that each of us has stepped up to a plan with all the "I's" dotted and the "T's" crossed and we were confident of success and it just didn't materialize. Devastated, however, if we are honest, we are able to look back and see why we made the choices we made and the blessings we derived from the setback. When we fail to do that, we will repeat the experiences over and over again without any growth.

Our growth comes when we are able to take accountability for what we did and take ownership in the lessons learned. Dismissing "failure" as merely a lesson learned, we can achieve a greater understanding of ourselves and our future if we seek to understand what we have gained from the experience. The lesson may very well be in the experience or it may be in the resulting detour. That is the blessing and the curse of detours. They provide great lessons and yet they can be hurtful along the way.

If we can learn to be thoughtful and reflective and respond like the wind-up toy that when it meets resistance it turns and redirects itself again and again. Eventually it finds the open ground and makes significant progress.

114

We, as people, hit the wall, fall to our knees, weep a bit, grovel a bit, pull ourselves up and force ourselves to move on in new directions. With the toy, there is no hesitation. It realizes it is not going to make any progress so it innately re-directs itself to try a new direction; it is very willing to take a detour. It goes until it finds new resistance and then redirects itself until it gains speed and the course is clear. How would our lives be different if we held the same level of mindlessness when we hit a wall or resistance and simply redirected ourselves with our eyes open to a new way of doing things? After all, if we knew that where we were going to end up is exactly where we were supposed to be, would it matter what course we took?

Letting go of having to proceed in a direct line will open the doors, open our eyes to the events and the happenings during a detour that might just be the journey desired. Of course if we had the ability to listen to the Inner Voice and act upon what we heard, there might be a greater chance of avoiding unnecessary detours.

In order for us to truly listen requires accountability and a tremendous degree of courage and faith. We first must have the willingness to take ownership of the part we played in manifesting the results we achieved. We have to have a willingness to look at our short sightedness and our blindness to the Inner Voice. Our ego took over. Our greed took over. Our pride took over. Quietly, the Inner Voice stands by and waits for us to "get it" and learn the power and the beauty of listening and following the voice within.

Sometimes the Inner Voice allows us or perhaps encourages us to take the detour so that we may better learn from our experiences. Doing so takes an enormous amount of faith and courage because we are going to be asked to do things that appear foreign and unfamiliar. We will resist the unknown and persist in ways that will eventually lead us to the detour. The Inner Voice may stand by and observe, waiting for the awakening. And further yet, the Inner Voice may actually encourage us to take the forbidden path because our faith is so weak, our courage so compromised.

I believe my experience of losing my house was clearly a message from my Inner Voice that said, "*I have tried to share with you that you don't need to own to enjoy but you have resisted, so I will lead you down that fateful path so that you might truly experience the pain and the personal growth that might lead to better understanding.*"

When the voice said, "*Keep going, stay the course,*" it was directing me down a path I had avoided for nearly 20 years. I fought it. I resisted it. I ignored it. The Inner Voice said, "*No more putting it off. The time has come.*"

That is the single most significant message I want to share with you: if you are reluctant to respond to the guidance of the Inner Voice out of fear and resistance to the journey, be ready for a more challenging journey fraught with more fear and pain than you had ever expected.

We are too easily diverted from our authentic journey out of fear and resistance to what we really want. Because we hold such importance on that which we truly love, we avoid seeking it so we don't have to face failure and disappointment. How ridiculous!

THE PRACTICE OF BEING

As you proceed through your day, take note of obvious detours. These are unexpected plans or obstacles that you were not expecting. What new things do you notice? What new awareness do you have? What events stimulate you to consider taking notice? Is there something odd or unusual that grabs your attention? What is that all about? What can you gain from that? What is the significance of what you see or who you meet?

Detours are the inconveniences
that take us in new directions
and teach us things that
we needed to learn,
to see but we couldn't or wouldn't
because we weren't ready or willing.
Timing is about detours where
when the time has come
for us to see the detour,
we choose of our own free will
to take the detour.

April 24, 2003
From The Author's Journal
Personal Insights from a Meditation

117

PERSONAL INSIGHTS

LET GO OF YOUR ATTACHMENT
TO THE OUTCOME

It may not be the final destination
but it certainly will lead us there.

Trusting the Inner Voice would be so much easier if we looked at it as a treasure hunt. With a treasure hunt, you don't really know what you are going to be doing and where it is going to take you. Surprisingly, we surrender to not knowing and accept it. We boldly step up and accept the challenge; we trust that we can handle each aspect of the game as it evolves. If we could only do the same thing with The Game of Life.

In life, we want assurances. We want guarantees. We want to know; we want it all planned out. Perhaps it is because we don't want to fail; failure, after all, is such a horrible stigma in our society. We allow our beliefs, our goals, our careers, our lives to be dictated by the fear of failure. And yet, we willingly accept the challenges of a treasure hunt and boldly go where no civil minded man would go in his own personal journey. We take risks, we accept defeat. We're okay with not knowing and not trying to figure out the outcome. We work attentively at the clues and the messages that come our way in hopes that it will clarify our path. But in life, this acceptance of messages and clues along the way often scares us. We want assurances that we don't expect in a healthy game of treasure hunt. Our egos are invested and our reputation is at stake. Consider, however, how different our lives might be if we didn't feel the shame of failure. In fact, imagine what life would be like if we celebrated our failures. Imagine a world that allowed each and every one of us to pursue our wildest dreams and fall flat on our face with a devastating defeat and respond with cheers and applause. That would be the celebration of letting go of the attachment to the outcome.

More so than the notion of letting go of the attachment to the outcome is the power of accepting that the outcome is for our highest good. It is difficult for many of us to perceive a painful outcome as a positive direction. We had clearly defined goals and expectations of something far greater; our dreams were squashed and our hopes flattened. When we are in the moment it is certainly challenging to see the positive, to see the value of the experience. When we let go of our attachment to the outcome, we release our need for our desired objectives to be that which we benefit from and we allow whatever transpires to be for our highest good, regardless of the outcome.

When I began building my home, the last thing I considered was potentially losing it to foreclosure or a lengthy court battle with the builder. That is an outcome that most people would avoid. However, it is, in many ways, a perfect outcome for me. While it has been extremely painful and devastating to both myself and my children, it has been an awakening for me to consider what is important in my life and free me to act in ways that would not have been made available to me.

This disastrous outcome has opened new doors for me that I would not have elected to open on my own. With my free will, my rational mind, my stories, my beliefs, I would have moved in an entirely different direction. Given the opportunity, I would not have acted in the same way that I have acted after experiencing this detour in my life. Not only is it a reason to celebrate because I tried to fulfill a dream I was passionate about and failed but it clearly moved me towards my right path. Wherever we go, we are there. Wherever our life takes us, it is our perfect destination. It may not be the final destination but it certainly will lead us there.

Having spent many years in the film industry, I have frequently considered writing a script about two identical twin brothers, Timothy and Henry, living in New York. Each share the same joy for life and the enthusiasm for theater. As children growing up they both dream of being actors. Yet, as they grow older and life meets them with responsibilities and choices to be made, Henry decides to pursue his passion for theater while Timothy realizes how challenging the success of that career can be and elects to become a financial planner on Wall Street. After all, isn't that where all the money is?

Years go by and Henry continues to hold down a job as a waiter and lives in a studio apartment. He often wonders if it is worth it. He squeaks by a living and earns enough money to pay his rent and take acting workshops and audition for minor roles in off Broadway plays. He has a steady girlfriend but has decided not to get married because of his financial situation. He'd like to have kids but it is the price he has determined he needs to pay.

Meanwhile, Timothy has worked his way up the ladder on Wall Street, earning a healthy six figure income. He and his wife and three children live in a comfortable suburban home outside the hustle and bustle of New York. His work keeps him very busy so he often has to forego attending his children's athletic events and school plays. After all, that is the price he has to pay to hold down such a stressful, time-consuming job. His health is compromised but he justifies it because, "That's just the way it is in this profession."

Still more years pass. Henry has had some success as an actor but he is considering giving it up and moving on with his life. His girlfriend moved to Los Angeles. He is alone, unsettled, frustrated and tormented by the lack of success he wanted to achieve as an actor.

Timothy, on the surface, is doing marvelously. He is now a partner with the firm and Vice President of Global Acquisitions. His children attend prestigious colleges and his wife, unhappy in their isolated marriage, is secretly having an affair. He has tickets to all the great plays that come to New York and often takes Henry because his wife has other plans. Both leave the theater with a sense of aliveness yet an undercurrent of sadness prevails as they discuss their lives. Neither feels that their lives are complete; something is horribly missing.

As they both approach mid-life, they ask themselves, "How did I get here?" Timothy discovers that his wife has been cheating on him for nearly ten years. He collapses one afternoon in the lobby of his office building and is rushed to the hospital for emergency by-pass surgery. There he lies in his hospital bed, neither his wife nor children by his side. He decides he needs to make a change.

Henry, having given up on acting, is now trying his luck with directing some off Broadway plays, and is beginning to feel passion again in his life. He gave up alcohol because it was getting the best of him. He is in a new relationship with the manager of a small theater; Melanie is nearly twenty years his junior. Henry and Melanie live in a modest flat, with a modest life, and a considerable degree of happiness. In fact, Henry is now quite content with directing and finds he is very talented at it; some say he has a great future as an up and coming New York director. He and Melanie are invited to many of the social gatherings. He continues to get praise for the work that he is doing; at forty-five, Henry's career is looking very promising. Henry couldn't be more elated when he learns Melanie is pregnant.

Meanwhile, Timothy returns to work. He pulls himself through the lobby into the elevator and climbs to the 39th floor where he is greeted by his personal assistant with a forced smile. He sits down at his desk and pulls the framed photographs of his children closer to take a deeper look. He sees happiness in their smiles; where had his happiness gone? He later learns that his division is under investigation and ultimately will lead to his financial ruin. Timothy ends up a broken man. He has no money. No home. No wife. His children call every weekend but he rarely sees them.

Timothy sees an advertisement in the local arts magazine for auditions for a play he did in high school. He decides on a whim to go down and try out. He gets the part. And the next part. And the part after that. Within two short years, Timothy establishes quite a name for himself as a very respected actor. He is recognized for his tremendous sensitivity and ability to express the internal turmoil of the characters he plays. Where did he develop that insight, you might ask?

Each man took a different path and through their life, their unique experiences, they were refined as they made new choices about the direction they were going to take. It matters not what choices you make and the attachment you might have to the outcome. Because in the end, if we are awake, we end up where we are supposed to be. It's following the path with faith. Taking one step at a time and allowing it to unfold. Make your plans, set your goals and step into them fully. In the end, let the outcome be the outcome. Wherever you are taken, it is so. Timothy took one path and Henry took another. In the end they ultimately ended up where they were supposed to be, regardless of their individual journey.

Letting go of your attachments is allowing your journey to unfold as naturally as possible. Let the current take you where it is going. Regardless of the choices or the goals we set, when surrendering to the outcome, we allow our perfect destiny to unfold. Who is to say how our choices influence our lives? I for one believe that with conscious effort and truly following the Inner Voice we end up where we were supposed to be regardless of the journey we take. When we don't listen, our journey may be more bumpy and take a little longer.

Our journeys may be different but removing the judgment or the attachment to the outcome, we are able to take the next clue to the treasure hunt and proceed to the end of the game: finding our authentic journey and living in peace and harmony within the world we have created.

THE PRACTICE OF BEING

When you make plans, set goals, let go of any attachments or expectations you might have with the outcome. Could you live with whatever happens? When the outcome is presented to you, can you identify how perfect it really is for your future development?

These last months leave me asking for assistance or guidance
on the issue of what I am supposed to do about making money.
So I asked again today. I listened. 'Play the lottery.'
Wow! Cool. That would solve all the problems.
This Inner Voice is so cool.
It has guided me to play the lottery.
Looks like my problems are over.
I'll be collecting a cool $33 million.
That should hold me over until my next big book deal.

December 27, 2001
From The Author's Journal
Personal Insights from a Meditation

I have bought lottery tickets for the last two weeks.
But the tickets come up, 'no winner.'
Frustrated and confused, I decided to go to the Source.
I posed the question,
'I thought I got a pretty clear sign to buy lottery tickets
as a solution to my money problems.
I specifically asked you what I should do
and you directed me to buy tickets.'
And with a flash I heard,
'Who said anything about winning the lottery?
It was a process.
Buying lottery tickets was a process for you to go through.
What did you learn?'
Wham. Where did that come from?

January 5, 2002
From The Author's Journal
Personal Insights from a Meditation

PERSONAL INSIGHTS

IT'S NOT LIKE RIDING A BIKE: ROUTINE IS ESSENTIAL

With each day of listening,
the voice becomes stronger,
more confident and more willing to respond.

I would, without a doubt, confess that the single greatest mistake I made in developing my connection to the Inner Voice was inconsistent practice. I started and stopped my meditation practice more times that I would like to recall. Perhaps it was laziness. Perhaps it was overconfidence. Perhaps it was my lack of belief that I had what it took. My inability to accept that my Inner Voice was as much a part of me as the color of my hair most likely distracted me from accepting the realness of this blessing. I think I questioned the power of this guidance and turned to my own abilities when my life was going well.

Oh, when life brought its challenges, I was quick to return to the power of the guidance that came from my Inner Voice. But once things got pulled together, I frequently forgot about the miraculous benefits that came with daily meditation. Because of these many false starts, I cannot emphasize enough the importance of routine. I have failed miserably at it. And even today, I find myself foregoing the practice of creating quiet space when my life gets full or my outer world appears pulled together. That commitment, that routine, has been my biggest challenge. I have paid a huge price as a result. Listening to the Inner Voice requires routine discipline. You cannot put the bike away and then pull it out and start where you left off. It doesn't work like that.

I have found that if I don't stay with a routine practice of listening for the still, quiet voice, it tends to be more difficult to call upon it after a period of absence. Knowing that, you would think I would stay to a schedule. And yet, in the thirty plus years of searching for the voice within, I turned my back on it when I felt I was doing okay without it. I would be a rich man if I paid myself a thousand dollars each time I apologized for my absence, my lack of discipline.

If it was like climbing back on a bicycle, maybe I wouldn't feel that way. But the frustration comes when I return to my practice of listening and I don't hear anything. I don't think the voice is spiteful. I think the voice operates best when it is exercised like a muscle and with repetition it becomes stronger. With absence, it becomes weaker and less toned. For it to respond, it needs your respect. Like a friend who leaves multiple messages on your answering machine, if you don't return the calls, they will stop calling. With each day of listening, the voice becomes stronger, more confident and more willing to respond. A broken routine leaves the voice out of touch with the line of communication.

With routine, a pattern is established and the voice begins to align itself with that routine. It is aligning itself with the synergy of your routine. Break that routine and the synergy is lost and the voice is more likely to become dormant. If you have ever started a paper or a thesis and then put it away for a while, it is extremely difficult to pick it back up and commence where you left off. It takes additional time to ramp back up again. You have to re-read what you have done to get back to where you were so you can continue. That is similar to the process with listening to the Inner Voice.

The re-connection is on more of a vibration level, however. It is reconnecting with the spirit on this path of Universal Energy. Let me try to explain. During a period of time that I was struggling with reconnecting to my Inner Voice, I entered a dry cleaner to pick up my clothes. For the first time I noticed the conveyer belt of clothes circled around the back of the room and then went up into the rafters, around the underside of a stairwell, back to the corner of the room, down again, across the room and back to the starting point.

I remember being impressed with how elaborate this continuous chain operated. What an efficient use of space and time, I thought. When I gave him my name, he pushed the toggle switch and the clothes rack began to circle around this maze designed to fill the space in this particular store, this unique environment. After one point, he reached the "g's" and stopped the conveyer belt. He mixed through the clothes and found an opening and deposited several hangers of newly cleaned clothes and then pushed the toggle switch once more. As he approached the "h's", he asked again the spelling of my name. Carefully, he searched the names as they went by until he came close to where he thought my clothes might be. He stopped the conveyor belt and one by one he pulled back the bundled clothes until he located mine and pulled them from the rack.

I paid my bill but remained in front of the counter because I was so intrigued with the idea that every bundle of clothes had it's perfect place upon this conveyor belt that weaved in and out of all corners of his store. It made me think that this is similar to the Universal Energy we live with each day. If we don't stay with the flow, if we don't connect at the right spot, we can be lost.

Finding order in the Universal Energy of life is what keeps us connected. There is an exact place where we fit into the order. This constant flow of energy circles around us and throughout our existence. Meditation or quieting the mind simply captures this Universal Energy as it circles by us. When we connect with the place in this energetic flow, our ride is perfectly ordained and we connect at a level many of us have experienced only a few times in our lives. It is where we are in sync with the whole order of life.

We find synergy when we stop and listen and find the place and time to connect and ride the Universal Energy. Quieting the mind and allowing us to tap into this energy is where we get our hits, our inspiration, our guidance. It is here and now and then it is gone. It has moved on.

That is why we often get different guidance because what is passing through us now is different from what is passing through us tomorrow or the next day or the years beyond. It flows around us, above us, beneath us, all around us. By listening routinely, we are better equipped to locate that specific place each time so that we can be in sync and synergy with the Universal Order. Without routine, it is like going into the dry cleaner without a ticket or a name and having to wait and search once more until the spot comes around so we can connect with it.

Once connected, we are now able to take the ride and go where the Universal Energy takes us. It's like the rope tow at a ski resort. We have our gloves wrapped around the tow line, allowing the rope to slip between our hands. When we feel it is the right time, we strengthen our grip and we lock onto that specific spot on the tow line that pulls us to the top. The results with listening to the voice within is like the rope tow. The more we listen and respond and seek our place in the order of the Universal Energy, the less rope has to pass through our hands before we are able to grasp the power of its energy.

THE PRACTICE OF BEING

Meditate each day for at least ten minutes. After each meditation, write down in a journal what you got from your mediation. After 21 days of doing this, look to see if your experience improved over time. Look at your last few entries. Then stop meditating for seven days and then resume meditation. See if you notice a break in the connectiveness.

This is so extremely frustrating!
I have had several days, even weeks of very consistent meditation
and the voice was becoming stronger and stronger.
The message seemed to be real.
I haven't meditated for a while and today
you would think that I had never meditated before in my life.
I got nothing.
Nothing.
I struggled and struggled to hear… to listen and I received no words,
no phrases, no images, nothing.
How can this be?

February 10, 1999
From The Author's Journal
Personal Insights from a Meditation

PERSONAL INSIGHTS

GOD IS LIKE
AN ANSWERING MACHINE

*Responding to the Inner Voice
strengthens the potency of the Inner Voice.
The more you feed and nourish it,
the more it feeds and nourishes you.*

Turning inward for answers is similar to turning on the answering machine. You turn on an answering machine to catch important messages while you are gone. When you have time, you play back the messages and take down what you need to know. That is almost identical to what the Inner Voice does. While you are caught up with life and living in an almost unconscious state, it makes itself available to you for insight once you take the time to check in. It tracks your life and takes down the important information and when you check in, it plays back what you need to hear. It plays that which needs to be said. It plays the message word for word, delicately connecting with the important and relevant information that needs to be communicated.

Often broken with silence, as with a sensitive caller who might be pondering his or her next words, similarly our Inner Voice may relay words in a broken pattern, searching for the truth. It doesn't change the message because it might be more appropriate or timely to do so. It plays the message when you demonstrate a need to hear the messages. If you don't turn within, it doesn't play the message. That is why I encourage meditating or quieting the mind regularly. That gives you an opportunity to listen to the messages. If you don't check your messages, you don't receive the information. If you don't check in with God, you don't hear the Inner Voice.

Like a good friend who leaves messages again and again, your Inner Voice does the same and wants the respect of a returned call. Over time, if your friend left dozens of messages and you didn't respond, they would likely stop calling. So is the same for the Inner Voice. One has to respond first by going within on a regular basis and secondly must take actions in response to the call. If your friend said she was going to write you a check but needed your address, without the act of returning the call, the results wouldn't happen.

If the Inner Voice calls you and suggests some action to take and you don't respond, there is a likelihood that the Inner Voice will become quieter and quieter. However, if you take the first step and begin to respond to the guidance of the Inner Voice, it becomes louder and louder and clearer and clearer and more and more routine over time. If you respond to your friend calling, it is more likely that they'll respond in kind. An exchange takes place. It becomes routine. It becomes natural.

In order to strengthen that relationship, responding is critical. As with the Inner Voice, over time with responding, the guidance may begin to come to you so subtly that it is almost like a fleeting thought; it may be inspired outside of the mechanics of meditation. Simply said, when you get into the practice of listening to the Inner Voice and responding to what you hear, you become more aware of its presence and you call upon the wisdom at random, outside of traditional meditation.

Tapping into that energy of the Inner Voice opens the door for you to receive more freely guidance that you may not have experienced in that way before. It only makes sense if you get used to settling in and connecting with that Inner Voice, out of habit, you might do that at other times in the day. A moment of reflection is now inspired. A thought or an idea might attract a reaction that guides you to move forward confidently. A scene of nature might invoke some clarity. When sleeping, you might enter a dreamlike state more frequently and draw greater connections with the messages from your dreams.

Even at times when we are oblivious, we are connected to the Universal Energy that connects to the spirit of the Inner Voice. We are all connected like the rack at the dry cleaners. There is a rightful place for each of us on the Universal Energy train. When we connect with the Inner Voice more regularly, we are able to squeeze tightly on the rope tow and connect to the Universal Energy that much faster and more naturally. In other words, responding to the Inner Voice strengthens the potency of the Inner Voice.

With more and more acts of faith, the voice comes more freely and in more subtle ways. At any given moment, the voice slips in and nudges you to make a call, run an errand, do a task. And you do.

That is what many would refer to as intuition. There is just this fleeting thought that you should act on something. That is the Inner Voice peeping its head out just enough that you get a sense about something. Intuition is just one aspect of the Inner Voice. It is joined by coincidences, gut responses, moments of brilliance, moments of awareness. These are all affirmations of the power of that Universal Energy fueled by the Inner Voice.

That's right. Each of us is a power source that feeds the Universal Energy. When we as a culture become less connected (otherwise distracted with greed and ego), the flow of the Universal Energy is affected adversely. That is why it is more important than ever that we seek a spiritual revolution at this time so that we can learn the power of tapping into the Inner Voice and fueling a more powerful, harmonious Universal Energy.

Our Universal Energy thrives and as it does, it connects and inspires us with subtle reminders that it is there; it feeds us that which we have fed. The more you feed and nourish your Inner Voice, the more it feeds and nourishes you.

The Inner Voice speaks to us in many ways. Answering the call is the most critical thing you can do. By being aware of the many ways the Inner Voice speaks to you, you are able to respond naturally and spontaneously and give the immediate feedback that you are listening. This acknowledgement of, "Thank you God" or simply, "thank you" makes that vital connection and restores and strengthens the relationship you have with your Inner Voice. This is an expression of gratitude. Gratitude builds the positive energy of the Universal Energy. Repeated gratitude locks the connection into place.

Struggling to feel that connection with the Inner Voice? Begin acknowledging and sharing gratitude for all the good things that are happening to you. Give thanks to the little nudges, the insights, the gifts, the coincidences that occur in your life on a daily basis. Begin to build the strength of your Inner Voice by simply being grateful. How simple is that? Get in the habit of saying, "Thank you, God" or simply, "Thank you." Acknowledge that the spirit resides in all things, is all around us, inside of us, above and below us.

These simple miracles can build into miraculous miracles by simply saying "yes." The Universal Energy will get used to the number of times you say "yes" and it will reward you with more and more experiences that deserve yet another "yes." If you want more yeses in your life, say more yeses. Show your appreciation, welcome the beauty and the greatness, and watch how your life will change.

A PRACTICE OF BEING

Throughout your day, when you feel the presence of God in your life, simply say, "Thank you, God". See if you notice a greater connection to your Higher Power when you acknowledge it on a regular basis.

Where did it go?
I can't believe I lost it.
But what has caused it to go silent?
Is it the part of the
'act now on what I have said.'
And when I do I will be rewarded with more messages.
I do not know.
I am confused.
I am frustrated.

February 18, 1999
From The Author's Journal
Personal Insights from a Meditation

PERSONAL INSIGHTS

THE WILLINGNESS TO BE

*What is most important is living in the moment
by listening to the Inner Voice right now
and finding peace in the now.*

I never thought it would be so difficult to shed the skin of my old self. Caught up with an ego and a drive, I lost track of who I was and began living a life of what I was. I measured myself by the car I drove, the money I made, the stature of my job, the notoriety of my career, the appearance of my family. Success was measured by "doingness." The more I did, the more I felt. The more I accomplished, the better I felt. The more satisfied I became, the bigger I felt. My feelings were based on what I did, what I do. It is easy to fall victim to this type of living because it is all around us. We experience this with our neighbors, we watch it on the television or read it in the paper. Our culture has taken us to what we have vs. who we are. Being. That takes a willingness to open the door, be vulnerable and Be. What does that mean, exactly?

"Beingness" is living your authentic journey. It is aligning your will with the will of your Higher Power. It is not about what you do but how you do it. It is about becoming one with your spirit. Listening to the Inner Voice connects you to that spirit. It is a journey and it is a process. It isn't easy to align yourself with your authentic journey. It may take years of struggle and frustration to bring you to what is important. Why is it that we have to be old, lying on our death bed, to realize what is important? Why can't we enjoy that peace of mind when we are young? We can. It requires tapping into your Inner Voice and connecting with your true being, regardless of how long it takes you to accomplish this.

Who you really are is not that which we see on the outside but what flows on the inside. Asking again and again for direction and clarity. Asking the Inner Voice to help you be a messenger. Because when we tap into that Inner Voice and we get the guidance we are seeking, it is not about me; it is about us, it is about the collective we. How can I do what I am intended to do on this earth and serve this society to my highest and best use? That is when the voice will answer. That is when the voice will guide you to get closer and closer to your authentic journey. Because when you are your authentic self, you are serving the Universal Energy and your soul is being fed daily.

You will discover that your authentic self is about "being." The emphasis is not on the doing but on the being. It comes in the form of service, not greed, not competition. It comes to you as genuinely and as pure as it can be. There is no judgment. There is no shame. There is no pressure. "Being" allows the Inner Voice to unfold new and dynamic aspects of your beingness that you have never been aware of. By simply "being," you invoke even more beingness. Opportunities appear, insights abound, coincidences become more frequent, and bliss follows.

Having the courage and faith to listen and act on the voice within only helps to elevate your passion for life. When we have experienced times where everything was going our way, we were in bliss. Remember to be thankful during these times. We often get caught up in the greatness of the moment and we fail to acknowledge how we got there in the first place. Taking that time to show your appreciation, to be grateful, is what fuels the good things to keep going. You are experiencing the flow. The flow of the Universal Energy in alignment with your Inner Voice.

But how do we protect ourselves from the trappings of the outer world? With all that goes on around us, the challenge is great to succumb to competition and comparison. There is a pretense that exists within our society that we must always be "fine." How are you? "Oh, I'm fine. I'm just great." When in reality, that might not be the case. We are driven to be our best, to put our best foot forward, to live a façade because it is the right thing to do.

In some cultures, the measurement of success is in your faith, not your possessions. In other cultures, they have chosen not to follow this hierarchy of needs. Instead, these cultures have aloud greed and ambition to drive their culture, to dictate their destiny and forget their history. And now, more than ever, we are being forced to reconsider. We are being forced to realign our thinking, our values. We were so much out of sync and synergy with the Universal Energy that now the rebalancing will be very painful for many. The rebalancing of the whole has forced the rebalancing of the self. The pendulum swung too far to one side and in order to obtain equilibrium it must swing to the far opposite side. Many will lose their homes, their life's savings, their identity. The pain will be great. But in the darkness, there will be light. It is in the darkness that we can see the light.

We can see where we have been and where we need to go. It is inevitable. It is necessary. It is so. We can fight it. Grieve it. Be angered by it. Or we can celebrate it. We can welcome the change, the rebalancing. The necessary flow of life, returning us to where we need to be. During these times, a person can share how they are truly feeling and, for once, there is the compassion and the sympathy that did not exist before. People didn't really want to hear it. Now, the authenticity of the spirit is returning. Genuine love and understanding is returning. Compassion and generosity is returning. We are coming home again. We are willing to be vulnerable. We are willing to be real. We are willing to be.

We are learning to Surrender. This concept is far more difficult that it appears. The idea of letting go and letting "what is, be what is" can be very challenging. It requires an incredible amount of faith and courage. Our minds want to wrap around "what is" and make it "what it is supposed to be."

Allowing the unusual or the unfamiliar to take precedence over the practical requires persistent reframing of the mind and the process of surrendering along the way. I know for myself, my process of thoroughly accepting what is was very trying. Programmed for years to believe that things need to be a certain way and play out in a rational manner prolonged my ability to accept each moment, each event, each setback as a matter of fact and accept it for what it was supposed to be.

Part of the magic of listening to the Inner Voice is accepting that "it is what it is." There is no changing it. There are no substitutions or variations. When the Inner Voice speaks, it is what it is and it requires the ultimate test of surrendering. Whether you understand the direction or accept the possible outcome is of no importance. The only important decision is to honor what you hear and step into it, regardless of the fear.

I compare this act of surrendering similar to what we are asked to do when we enter a new relationship. There are no guarantees. There are no assurances that the steps we take or the time we invest, will result in the optimum outcome that we seek at the time of entering the relationship. We can only trust that the moment we have in the here and now is precious and worth continuing. We cannot speculate on the outcome or dictate the destination. We can only accept each day as a day well spent with our new partner. Worrying about the outcome will only distract from the moment.

This will be challenging for many as they look to their empty checking accounts at the end of the month. They will be challenged to live in the moment and not be angered by the past or fearful of the future. But spending precious time fully present in the now is far more imperative than focusing on the doubt or fears about the eventual outcome. If the now is working, keep living the now. If the now is not working, surrender and know that the now, in the future, will bring us to exactly where we are supposed to be. It's all good. It's all perfect. It is all rebalancing and finding our alignment with the Universal Energy.

It has always amazed me how people feel more connected to someone that is willing to be vulnerable and share intimate details about their lives. One would think that there would be judgment and the fear of rejection if you shared an intimate truth about the frailties of your personality. It's scary to most and that is why we hold back and refrain from sharing openly. The fear is too great so the façade of our persona is projected. This false preposition of guarding your personality against adverse discovery is far more damaging than surrendering and allowing yourself to be vulnerable. By opening up to being vulnerable, you open up to the acceptance and the truth we all seek so desperately.

By exposing our inner secrets, we release the guards at the door and allow all to enter, including the powerful influence of the voice within. It is far more difficult to receive the lessons from the Inner Voice if you are defending your right to hold back the truth and avoid vulnerability. After all, what is there to hide? You will be loved and appreciated for being, being real, being vulnerable, being you.

A very good friend of mine opened his heart and shared his pain with me over the loss of his wife to cancer, "When one chooses to love, they choose to feel pain. When one steps into a commitment to love someone fully, there is always a decision to accept pain in their life. If one fully loves, regardless of the fear of the outcome, they will experience pain by either ending the relationship prematurely or experiencing the death of their partner."

That is why so many people go into relationships guarded; they want to avoid the possibility of getting hurt when the relationship ends. How often do we look at the relationship with the intention of it being the most beautiful, ever-lasting, "storybook relationship" that has ever been imagined? The movie, *The Notebook*, is one such example of everlasting love. Yet, when we are holding back and playing it safe, have we not considered that this is perhaps the relationship we seek? And if that is the case, have we considered the pain that will come when the love of our life dies before we do? Either way, a decision to love is a decision to accept that pain is a part of the deal. If we choose to live our life, pain is a part of the deal.

When we accept life as a choice to live and be, we must welcome the resulting pain and celebrate what we can gain from its presence in our lives. Why then worry about the future?

Why be stressed? Why fear the tomorrows and sadden our todays? Isn't it far more rewarding to live the relationship (of life) in the moment, knowing that with a failed relationship or an exemplary relationship of love and devotion, there will be an experience of pain. So is the same commitment to listening to the Inner Voice.

With the acceptance and the devotion to the inner knowing, there is no guarantee of the outcome and certain consequences may just be a part of the formula. Why worry about the future when what is most important is living in the moment by "listening" to the Inner Voice right now and finding peace in the now. If we hear the powerful words of the Inner Voice and we speculate on how it will take us to pleasure or pain, we defeat the whole purpose of listening to the voice within. Rather, we are much better poised to experience the "glorious success of the (inner) spoken word" when we dispense any attachment to the outcome and celebrate the moment of now.

As in the eventual outcome of a relationship, why waste the beauty of each day's bliss by worrying about whether it is going to turn out the way we believe it should. Is the relationship a blessing that is intended to help us expand or grow in a certain way, without regard to the outcome? Is the Inner Voice a blessing that is intended to help us expand and grow in a certain way, without regard to the outcome? Is life a blessing that is intended to help us expand and grow in a certain way, without regard to the outcome?

Surrender is a powerful thing. It is the letting go of the outcome and accepting the present with as much vulnerability for the truth as humanly possible. Let down the guard and allow the voice to come forth. With the humility of letting go of pretenses, we prepare ourselves to hear the Inner Voice, to act with confidence, to remain disciplined with daily practice of going within, and living a blessed life, day by day by day.

A PRACTICE OF BEING

When life throws you curve balls that bring you pain and sorrow, surrender, and share your thoughts and feelings opening with a loved one. Be still and listen to the voice within where you will find peace and acceptance with where you are at at that given moment. That moment is now gone and you have opened yourself to experiencing a precious new moment, full of new opportunities and expressions of love and security.

It is not in a happy and contented way
That we truly grow.
Sorry to break your bubble.
But life is not all about joy and happiness
And walking in a fog of bliss.
It is a journey of self discovery that does require
the pain
To go deep within and learn that which
we would not have done otherwise.

April 23, 2003
From The Author's Journal
The Inner Voice

PERSONAL INSIGHTS

PERSONAL INSIGHTS

LOOK AT LIFE
FROM A WHOLE NEW PERSPECTIVE

*The life we are living right now is the perfect life
we are supposed to be living.
Where we are at is just the period of time before
where we are going.*

It takes courage to wake up to your life and be willing to accept what role you played in making it as you did. The choices that we have made all these years play out for us in a physical form that illustrates clearly the good choices we have made and the bad choices. The difference between the conscious choices and the unconscious choices.

Without the guidance of the Inner Voice, we often find ourselves making choices we believe are in our best interest but they are clouded by past experiences, obligations and responsibilities of the time, beliefs from our parents and the journey we have embarked on. So much of what we decide to do is based on practical, rational, reasoning based on a foundation flawed with misconceptions or combative fears and beliefs. How then is it truly possible for us to make good decisions without the divine intelligence of the Inner Voice?

And yet that is what we have done again and again. We have turned to our imperfect intellect to make decisions in our life. We have trusted that the outcomes will bring us the rewards we have been looking for. At times we are successful and at others we are not.

Imagine that you have within you a validator extrordinaire that can respond to your thoughts with astute awareness of what is best for you. Wouldn't that be reassuring? Wouldn't that be liberating? After all, if that were the case, we could step more fully into living an incredible life because there is no reservation about making a bad decision. But again, I must remind you that there are no guarantees. There is no absolute assurance that the Inner Voice will take you to your immediate outcome. There may be lessons to be learned, insights to be acknowledged or blessings to be celebrated. Tapping into your Inner Voice simply opens the runway for the landing of your life's progressions.

Unconsciously, many of us have reached a point in our life where we can't believe we have placed ourselves in such a mess. How could we have made such bad choices? By being accountable and willing to look at the situation with humility, one can better derive guidance from the Inner Voice. By being able to pinpoint the specific decisions you made that might have been unhealthy or inappropriate for you, you are then better prepared to go to that Inner Voice and ask for direction.

It is in the vulnerability of our character that allows us to reap the benefits of the guiding Inner Voice. This acceptance or accountability removes the pretenses and allows the real awakening to begin. Ignorance and denial will not feed the spirit of the Inner Voice. Vulnerability and forgiveness will. Acknowledging our errors and letting them go creates space and movement for the Inner Voice to redirect. Without this acceptance, it is very hard for the Inner Voice to penetrate the soul and transform the spirit with new insight. Preparation for a better tomorrow is thwarted. Time is prolonged. Uncertainty festers. By surrendering to our own ignorance, we open the doors for the Inner Voice to scream with clarity and take us where we need to go.

Knowing that our Inner Voice is poised to help us move in the right direction, we must know that everything is going to be all right. Take that in and be with that. Imagine if we were assured that everything was going to be all right. Not just all right but phenomenal.

Live life from the perspective that the Inner Voice can and does guide us when we get in a habit of listening and it takes us where we are supposed to be, regardless of the route we take. When we can really get there, then life is bliss. When we can *accept* that the life we are living right now is the perfect life we are supposed to be living, then we ought to be very motivated to tap into the Inner Voice and say, "Guide me from here." Know that where I am is perfect. Everything is perfect. Everything falls in your path for very specific reasons. There are no accidents. Life is constantly searching for equilibrium. The pendulum swings from right to left to keep us in balance. With the disappointment comes the blessing. With darkness comes the light.

There is no accident that the collaborative efforts of mankind have caused us to swing back into balance with the here and now. We were caught up with the external world, what lies ahead, searching, planning, looking ahead. We lost touch with "living in the moment." But with this global rebalancing of our financial institutions, more and more of us are forced to focus in the moment, day by day. Instead of planning for bigger things to come, this rebalancing is forcing us to think about today. We have brought in our sights and we are looking more to where we are at in this moment of time. This upheaval is forcing us to return to where we are supposed to be. Lost in our greed and drive for success in the material world, we are being redirected back to the values that make us strong and give us peace of mind, peace of spirit.

In the moment, accept where you are and claim, "it is all perfect." For when we live in the moment and give thanks for the present, we open up the Universal Energy to feed us with abundant living. Not abundance as in money but abundance as in all things are possible. All things come from one thing. Where we are at is just the period of time before where we are going. It is not to be revered as hopeless or pathetic but of opportunities abounding for the coming of tomorrow. All will be revealed when the lessons are learned and the awakening has taken place.

It wasn't too long ago that I had it out with God. Here I was in the middle of this book espousing my wisdom about listening to the power of the Inner Voice and my life seemed to be crumbling around me. How could I preach this knowledge and feel so unconnected to the Source? So in a meditation I asked my Inner Voice why I was being tested so severely. This inquisition turned into a rant and I let God have it; under no uncertain terms, I wanted my Higher Power to know that I was upset, fed up, worn out, torn down, beat up, and discouraged beyond measure. I ranted and raved for several minutes, venting my frustration and anger towards the events that were appearing in my life.

In the end, I sat quietly and to my surprise a peace of mind came over me like I had never experienced before. A wave of gratitude filled my body and fed my soul. I was at peace; I fully accepted where I was and what was happening to me and the powerful lessons I was learning. Gratitude abounded. And I spoke out loud, "Thank you, God."

That is not what I expected. I did not expect this wave of peace and this level of contentment to ease my hurt, calm my spirit and bring me reassurance that everything was going to be all right. I guess I knew that my Inner Voice was speaking to me. That's when you know. You know when there is a peace of mind; there is reassurance that the steps you are taking are the right ones or the ones you need to take are just before you.

The steps we take, with support from the Inner Voice, feel right; they rarely are met with fear. At some level, we know they are the right steps to take. We can tackle just about any obstacle and overcome most adversities with an assurance that everything is going to be all right because we experience the action steps with a peaceful reassurance unmeasured by the calculating mind. There is a big difference between taking a risk influenced by the mind and the risks we take with the reassurance of the Inner Voice.

Things don't just happen as an accident. There is a plan. A plan far greater than ourselves. There is balance and there is re-balancing. Each and every thing that happens to us is preparing us for something better. These things are not just random acts with no purpose or intent. They are specific and with great intent. Each life event, whether good or bad, deserves a moment of reflection. A moment to see how this piece of the puzzle is directing you in your life. Not to be treated as insignificant, each event is intended to open the door to the next segment of our journey.

We have many choices and sometimes we don't know which choice to make. It doesn't really matter. Each choice leads us to where we are supposed to go-back to finding our authentic journey. No matter what door we choose, the path, whether direct or blessed with detours, will eventually take us to our final destination.

I recall this scene from a comedy skit where people are in a corridor with multiple doors. Searching. Searching. There are so many doors to choose, which one is the right one? They enter one only to come out of another back into the corridor. They try another door only to return.

That is life. We have choices and we make the best of them. Some work well and some lead us back to our path and we try another doorway. When an event happens in our life, consider that we are in the corridor, moving about, giving consideration, and then selecting a new door to enter. There is no judgment about the place that we are at in the corridor. There is no judgment about the door we choose because, in the end, we will end up exactly where we need to be. The corridor is simply a holding station until we get ourselves grounded and take a new path by making a choice and opening the door.

The Inner Voice, when conferred with, will help you choose a door that is ultimately designed to take you where you are supposed to go. Without consulting the Inner Voice, you may just spend more time in the corridor searching for the right door. And that doesn't mean you won't return to the corridor another time to reflect and make another choice.

True happiness comes when we don't put pressure on ourselves by labeling where we are at when we are in the corridor.

154

It makes no difference. The corridor is neutral. No judgment. No anxiety. No nothing. You are just there to prepare yourself for the next segment and to find your authentic journey. Being confused or lacking direction is perfectly okay. You are simply in the corridor awaiting guidance on which door to take. Your journey will be full of bliss and wonderment, and the corridor always available, always providing abundant wisdom of the here and now.

A PRACTICE OF BEING

When you find yourself stressed and anxious about your future, surrender and be content in the here and now. Know that where you are is perfect and the path you will take is perfect. No need to worry. You are on your rightful path that will bring you great blessings of peace and joy. Listen. Suspend judgment. Trust what you hear in the moment. Act on it.

How willing are you to look at the truth
and accept it?
Are you willing to accept that you
could play a major role in this century
with discovering the truths of who you are
and how to find peace within?
Does that settle with you?

"Yes, I'm okay with it but why does it have to be such
A big thing?
Why can't it just be an Ordinary guy
doing an ordinary thing?"

155

Is that not what you want
so that you can make a big difference?
Before it was ego.
Now that it is gone.
Is it not that you want to make a big difference?
To have the power or the influence
To step up and make a difference.

"So you are saying that I can step into it and reach out there
to speak the truth and say things that
people may or may not be willing to hear and
I will not be punished for it?"

You will not only not be punished but
you will be rewarded.
You will have such great satisfaction from the things you do and
the words you speak.
Thousands will appreciate your honesty and truth
And listen to your words
And be inspired.

April 16, 2003
From The Author's Journal
Talking with The Inner Voice

PERSONAL INSIGHTS

PERSONAL INSIGHTS

IT CAN GO
BOTH DIRECTIONS

In prayer, we talk to God.
In meditation, God talks to us.

I was living and working in Southern California with lots of extra time on my hands. I had taken a job in hopes it would land an opportunity for my family to relocate to the sun. I thought I had temporarily left my wife and two children behind in Oregon to launch a new career. Was I in for a surprise? What little I knew. My office was on Hwy 101 in San Juan Capistrano. My desk had an uninterrupted view of the beach, the palm trees and the evening sunsets over the Pacific Ocean. Life couldn't get any better. I often worked late and took a final stroll on the beach before the sun went down and then returned to my office. I was finishing a script so I spent many long evenings pounding away at the keyboard.

One night I decided it would be fun to start a journal. I commenced writing. Then it happened. The Voice called out, *"Write!"* So I decided that I would take a run at writing to God and see if I would get a response. At first, it was very awkward. I didn't really know what to do. I typed a question and sat. Nothing happened. I didn't know what to expect. I typed another question and closed my eyes. Immediately a word came to mind and I impulsively typed the word. Immediately another word came into my mind so I typed it. And again and again and I had a sentence. Soon I had a paragraph. I didn't really know what I was writing; it was if I was unconscious.

Here are the first paragraphs I wrote the night of January 20, 2003:

"It is not enough to feel the pain within. It must be experienced at a deeper level that gets to the core of who we are. For it is through the pain in our lives that we truly discover our greatness and prosper in the world of knowing. It is in this world of knowing that we truly release ourselves of the pain and the restraints that hold us back. Deep down we know. We all know. We just resist it because it scares us that we should have such power. Who am I to feel such power? Know that power resides in all of us and it is here that we find freedom, freedom of doubt and disparagement. Trusting the voice is the challenge because it is new and foreign. Trust, however, its power and you shall be set free."

What? You got to be kidding me! That came out of me? Where did that come from? I will always remember that night; it was the most amazing experience one could ever imagine. I went on to write almost every night. I accumulated dozens and dozens of pages of writings. Again, more insights:

"Start with what you know and allow what you don't know to appear. Do not be surprised or scared. Allow it to come freely and do not pass judgment. You have something to share and you must go forth now and share it. Be strong for there will be opposition and doubt

and criticism. You must believe and know that what you are doing is right and divinely guided."

"Will you help me, guide me in a way that I will truly know?"

"It is in my hand that I shall guide you. Take a step and the guidance will be there. Remember to look back and observe your steps because they shall be mighty. Look forward for the journey will be bright. The journey will be long and fruitful."

"When I get scared or feel the doubt and want to flee, what should I do?"

"Trust. Trust the process."

"But how long can I go on trust? I need to feel confident and assured that I am on the right path and not making an idiot of myself."

"You will know because the words will be so powerful you cannot deny them. The strength of the word will lead you forward. Trust in yourself and the wisdom passed down to you from Karma."

"What do you mean by Karma?"

"Karma is your mother and she gave you birth but she is the knowing but doesn't know it and you are her messenger."

"I already doubt that. I feel I am wanting to tell

myself that, not that it is really true. I am thinking I am crazy. This is so far fetched."

"What makes it far-fetched? That you are finally listening to the voice within that you have wanted to hear for many years. So now I am present. Why do you turn your back?"

"I'm scared."

"So what did I tell you about being scared?"

"Trust?"

"Right. Surrender, Mark. You've asked for this journey; it has arrived. Enjoy the fruits of your journey that has brought you this far. It is glorious and you shall be rewarded."

I was becoming more and more alarmed at what was coming of my writing. How so ironic that I wanted this ability to show itself but when it did I couldn't handle it. The fear and doubt crept in. On January 23, 2003, I wrote,

"So I can't help it. The doubt creeps in so I start to think of tough questions to ask to get a bad response so I can say, ' see, this is a hoax'."

I continued to write and listen. Now the tides turned and the Inner Voice starting asking me questions:

"Notice how I am now asking you questions and you are answering. Before, you took the wisdom and the

knowing from me. You are now on the track of pulling the knowing automatically. The voice is speaking and you are responding. So Mark, once again, where does this leave you? Where and how do you want to focus your attention."

"I want to focus on . . . the area of clairvoyance and natural knowing. All my writings, my movies, my speeches should go in that direction."

And so began the evolution of my exchange of dialogue with God, my Inner Voice. It began years earlier with a directive to, *"Go write,"* but I didn't follow through because the time was not right. I did not believe that I was entitled to write on such a topic. However, I continued my journey and it led me to unfolding my Divine Intelligence through the written word.

Not only did I gain by writing what I thought, it opened me up to hearing what God thought. My writing opened the doors so that I could talk to God and God could talk to me.

Years passed and a time came when I wanted to test this relationship through meditation. I put myself in a quiet place and sat still. I remained still for some time. Then I asked my first question. A word came to me so I spoke it out loud. Another word came so I spoke it. Again and again, just like the writing. I trusted that the words would form sentences and the sentences would form thoughts. And they did.

Over time, I have developed a comfortable relationship with my Inner Voice and we speak often. I no longer consider it odd or out of the ordinary. I consider it quite ordinary. It is a routine part of my life. And because I dispelled the myth that I have to be special to hear the Inner Voice, I decided it was time to share that with others.

Whatever your journey, whatever steps you take, and the time it takes to get there, the search for the Inner Voice is a worthy one. The first step is believing that it is as natural as taking in breath. It is as ordinary as talking on the phone. In prayer, we talk to God. In meditation, God talks to us. Isn't it nice to know that we can talk to God and God will talk back. It's all in the beauty and the bewilderment of trusting our journey to be a perfect one and living each moment with the deepest faith that you know it to be true.

A PRACTICE OF BEING

Sit quietly. Be still. Allow the thoughts of the day to drift away. Listen. If a word comes to you, say it out loud. Follow it with other words that come to mind. Allow it to form a question if it will. After speaking out loud, listen. Listen. If you hear or sense a word, speak it out loud, followed by the next word that comes and continue until you feel you have heard what you are supposed to have heard. The Inner Voice might tell you it is done or it might just be still and you can't pick up any more words. Ask another question if you would like. Listen. Respond out loud with that which you hear. Continue to do this. Continue the routine. Continue to trust and let it flow. Get in the habit of doing this on a daily basis. Enjoy the bliss.

What I have to caution you about is that it is not
one common voice for everyone.
Since the power is within each of us
and owned by each of us individually,
then the voice is individually unique.
It is not a common voice,
a single presence that speaks to all.
In fact, the differences help to support that there is the
singular power within each and every one of us.
It is the voice that is uniquely our own,
speaking in tones and styles that belong to us.

When I quiet myself further and take several deep breaths
and totally relax my mind and allow any and all
thoughts or feelings to come, that's when I begin to hear
the voice that comes from another place.
Whether it's coming from my heart, my mind, or my gut.
It is a voice that speaks one layer away from my being.
What does that mean, I do not know.
The words come and I know they are the words of
My Higher Power.
I often speak out loud by asking the questions
I seek answers for or give thanks for its presence.
I hear, in return, a response.
I have found most effectively, for me, is to speak those words
Out loud as well.
Soon I am in a dialogue with myself.
It's almost as if I am playing chess by myself.

From The Author's Journal
Personal Insights from a Meditation

PERSONAL INSIGHTS

I DON'T NEED
TO BE SPECIAL

*Accepting the ordinary
has made my life most
Extraordinary.*

My greatest self-defeating pattern was falling victim to the belief that I was a fake. That my ego wanted me to be special but, in reality, I wasn't. I wasn't anything special; I was quite ordinary, to my disappointment. I wanted to hear the Inner Voice but I didn't believe it was possible. Over the years, I questioned my ability and my authenticity. I wondered if it was more of a desire for my ego than my spirit.

I couldn't get past the idea, the possibility, that being able to hear the voice within was just no big deal and that everyone had the ability. Why make such a fuss about it? Why couldn't I accept it as normal?

I couldn't comprehend that the ability to tap into the Inner Voice and call forth this great wisdom was quite ordinary. I somehow had it firmly embedded in my mind that the "gift" of listening to the Inner Voice and being able to call forth it's wealth of knowledge was only attainable to those that were special. I convinced myself again and again that I was making this all up. That this new insight into my inner psychic was hopefulness at best. I wanted to believe. I wanted to think that it was real, that it was true. Yet, I tested it repeatedly and sure enough I found solid reasoning that I was fabricating this whole thing. I just wanted to feel special.

But, with the passing of time and the lessons learned, I have come to believe that it is quite the opposite. I didn't need to be special. I could be quite ordinary and share this same gift with those spiritual teachers that had discovered it before me. I came to appreciate that I didn't need to be special to tap into that Inner Voice and receive the guidance that would set me free.

Each time, it was at that very point when I accepted it as routine that the voice became stronger and stronger. It was at those points in my life that I accepted this ability to be as common as singing a song, writing a verse, drawing a picture, or speaking from the heart. It was no different. It did not require any additional training or expertise. It was as natural as all other aspects in my life.

I didn't question that I had a gift for connecting with people. I didn't question that I had a predisposition for taking risks and doing so effortlessly. I didn't question myself for my knack of speaking in front of groups with a style that left people inspired. So why would I question the idea that I can quiet my mind, center myself, focus my energy on my inner soul and hear a guiding voice that knew my truth? In my earlier days, I would have found that outlandish and arrogant.

Today, I see it as ordinary as taking a walk. That acceptance has done more for me in untapping the Inner Voice than any workshop or CD that professes the answers to enlightenment. Accepting the ordinary has made my life most extraordinary. I believe once we dispel the myth we have to be special to hear the Inner Voice, we have accomplished our greatest hurdle in welcoming the calming spirit of that Inner Voice. Accepting that it is real, it is attainable, it is ordinary. It brings you to the place you need to be to hear that voice. At that point, it simply reveals itself.

I have written about my first experience of hearing the Inner Voice when I heard, *"You don't need to own to enjoy."* Because it was new, it was foreign, I locked into what that voice sounded like. I spent years trying to duplicate the tone, the quality, the clarity, the flow of the words. After all, when you hear something you feel is that remarkable, you want to wrap it up in its very special wrapping paper and hold firm its presentation.

So without knowing, I set myself up to miss other clues, other nudges, other communications because I was fixed on what it looked like and what it sounded like. I went for years forcing myself to get back to that tone, that feeling I experienced that day, years before.

I'm not sure I have heard that same voice more than a half a dozen times. It makes sense, however, that I wouldn't because it was new, it was foreign. I wish I could compare it to the first kiss or the first insight or the first time I heard a foreign phrase or unfamiliar word, but I can't. Because it was so impressive, I don't know (and I now don't expect) that it may ever be the same. I would suspect that it might be close to hearing your child speak for the very first time. The beauty and the miracle of their first word. With the passing of time, those spoken words are not so special, not so miraculous, yet they hold the same power as they did when spoken the very first time.

In the end, I have grown to understand the miracles of the Inner Voice coming to me in many different ways. I don't need the amazing impact of the voice to recognize it.

With the passing of time, it has become more subtle, more quiet, more calming, more common. Perhaps I have accepted the awesomeness of the experience as an ordinary process with the words being spoken as if they were my own. And that is the miracle of listening to the voice within. It begins with a sense of miraculousness and wonderment and transforms into quite the ordinary, the accepted, the norm.

Now the voice comes to me in a conversational style. Nothing dramatic. Nothing unordinary. Nothing remarkable. The Inner Voice is now more like a very good friend. This new friend knows me better than anyone. This new friend has the wisdom of ages. This new friend is patient, understanding, calming, and reassuring. This new friend knows what is best for me and wants to support my getting there. This new friend speaks without judgment and without obligation or guilt. This new friend is genuine and honest. And this new friend demands that I be diligent with my commitment.

If I falter, if I minimize, if I ignore, if I don't respond, my new friend will be less available to me. And I have learned that, many times in my life, and I do not want that. Like all relationships, we have to commit to nurturing them in order to get the very best from them. I speak to God each and every day.

It is a different way of communicating. It is a mutual understanding. A knowing. A being... together as one. I talk to God and God talks to me. I listen and respond instinctively. I am grateful. I take the time to quiet my mind, listen to my soul, and hear the blessings that are bestowed upon me. What I do every day is give thanks. To live in gratitude for the voice that comes to me at the stop sign, in the grocery store, as I take my walk.

God is all around us. Accepting this new friend as ordinary will only enhance the guidance in your daily life. Your new friend will visit you in the most unusual places at the most unusual times.

Welcome it as ordinary and real and you will be on your way of dispelling the myth that you have to be special to gain the power of your inner knowledge and guiding spirit.

It has been a long, hard journey and my wish for you is that you experience something entirely different. I wish for you that you accept that you don't have to be special; you are enough and your Inner Voice awaits your call.

A PRACTICE OF BEING

Be Still. Let go of any attachment to an outcome. Listen. Have faith and courage. Respond. Take baby steps. Accept that where you are is perfect. Meditate regularly. Demonstrate gratitude. "Thank you, God." See the lessons in all things. Surrender. Look within. Listen. Speak. Listen. Speak the words you hear. Give thanks. You don't need to be special to hear the Inner Voice.

"Mark, you must go do what you must go do.
You cannot wait or put it off any further.
It's suffocating you.
You are dying a slow death with procrastination.
Act now.
Find the pace, find the path and run with it.
Don't hesitate and meander.
Get in the Rhythm,
The Alignment,
And Go For It, Now."

January 29, 2004
From The Author's Journal
Talking with The Inner Voice

PERSONAL INSIGHTS

PERSONAL INSIGHTS

EPILOGUE

When I was directed to write, to write this particular book, I responded to the voice within as I do with all my guidance. I just acted upon it. As I am directed to make a phone call, complete a task, take some action, I just began to write. Little did I know that during the writing of this book we would begin to experience the greatest economic meltdown in the history of the world. I did not give consideration to the topic or the content of this book because of what was happening around me. Again, I focused on that which was happening within me.

I gave little consideration to the impact this book might have on the lives of those individuals that were losing their homes to foreclosure, fighting the daily challenges of unemployment or the loss of their retirement, or the struggle they might have with their faltering faith in the system around them. I just wrote.

I just dedicated myself to be in the moment; I aspired to be in the here and now as I allowed the Inner Voice to guide me with the words I needed to write. I gave little consideration to the marketability of the book. I cared not if one or one million would benefit. I invested my energy with that which I thought was right for me at the time. I directed my inner guidance to listen to the thoughts that flowed from me not to me.

It was somewhere around the early 1990's that I was first inspired to write this book and it wasn't until 2008 that I made the commitment to follow through. To act upon my guidance. To step into the knowing of what my Inner Voice had been calling me to do for nearly twenty years.

I think of the preparation I went through to write this book. It's all in the timing. The pain and the struggle. The happiness and the grief. The good times and the bad. The ups and downs. The glorious times and the pathetic times. It has all been in preparation; it is all in the timing. I experienced the pain of a divorce, the exploration of a career in real estate and life coaching, loss of my home, raising two children as a single parent, lessons of letting go of attachments, commitment to listening to the voice within, and began the witnessing of a global economic collapse. Why now? Why now has all this evolved to a point and time for me to write this book?

It is all in the preparation. We cannot dictate the timing. The moment in time comes when the moment is right. We cannot squander lost opportunities or fret over wasted time; it is all in the preparation of something better for us. Be patient. We all have our journeys and we all are being prepared for something greater than ourselves.

Nothing, and I mean, nothing, is brought to us as incidental: it all has a significant meaning and place in our lives. Maybe not in that particular moment but in a moment in time, the lessons we have learned will be there so we can be of service and give what we have learned. There is no accident that my work as a realtor took me to exploring ways of helping those that were losing their homes to foreclosure while I explored my understanding of the spirit within, the Inner Voice, and began my work as a life coach. There are no accidents that I lost my home to the fate of another's failure to be honest—that my life was blindsided by those who hold little integrity for doing the right thing.

It has all been a giant lesson in surrendering and finding what is important: the tranquility and solitude of the magic of the Inner Voice. Finding the God within. Connecting to a Universal Energy. What better way to explain the influence of the Universal Energy than demonstrating how it realigns us as individuals and collectively as a world society. As in the past, we are not experiencing an industrial revolution, we are experiencing a "spiritual evolution".

It is not something happening around us, it is something happening within us. It is the evolution of our spirit within us, commencing from within and expanding out—evolving from the inside out, from the Source.

When we can't trust what is happening outside our doors, we certainly have the power to trust what is happening within our gates. This evolution is all part of the cosmic readjustment that the Universal Energy is calling for. This Universal Energy has determined the time is now to realize that the natural flow of life is far greater than the ownership of real estate or the attachment to stuff that we own. I have certainly gone through a major transformation. An awakening. A new way of thinking, a new way of Being.

It is in this Being that we as a society must come to honor. Step into it in our own way. Be who we are uniquely to "Be" by listening and being open to the natural flow of the order. As the Science of Karma suggests, "Every action has an equal and opposite reaction," and our society, our world, is simply going through a rebalancing... a readjustment of values. This rebalancing may require the pendulum to swing to the far side and with it will come pain and heartache. It, unfortunately, is necessary to bring us back to who we are.

Our world is going through a re-evaluation. We are questioning the greed that has fed so many of us all these years. We are questioning our values with family vs. work, status vs. comfort, wealth vs. happiness, and being vs. doing. We are awakening to the lost years of doing what we thought we ought to be doing vs. being who we are. We got caught up in the glamour of success and lost sight of the joy of the moment and the pleasure of knowing the peace that resides within us. We are a culture that lost ourselves in the wave of opportunities and forgot to consider the simple things in life like family and friendship. We pushed ourselves to be great, to reach pinnacles of success by doing things we know we shouldn't. We lost sight of the integrity of a kind word, a helping hand, a deed done for the benefit of all. We surrounded ourselves with notions and potions for a false happiness and forgot to remember the glory of the journey.

There is a lot to be considered, much to be re-evaluated... a daunting task. The rebalancing will be painful and the journey dark at times but it is necessary. We must pull back and consider what is wise, what is prudent. We must return to values that built character rather than tore it apart. We have allowed ourselves to build our character by the size of our billfold or the depths of our holdings. We have developed an attachment to who we are by what we own.

And now, with much of that disappearing for millions,

we are at our greatest challenge: to reclaim who we are rather than what we do or how we are measured by what we own. We cannot allow our despair to dictate the quality of our character. It is a time to help our neighbors. Give a hand to those in need. To connect with our families and together raise children with lasting values. It is time to make a deal that works for all: To think about our world before we think about our wealth. Reach out. Expect random acts of kindness by initiating them on our own. To lift up. To follow our hearts. Listen to our Voice. We must go within to find the peace and the harmony and the greatness of this exact moment in time.

There is a rebalancing. There is a readjustment taking place. It is all for the good. It is necessary. It is right. It is now. No changing that. We can't hide from the truth or turn our backs on reality. Now is the time to reach to a higher level by going to our Higher Power. We cannot seek solutions to our dilemmas with the taking of our life, but rather the raising up of our life. The rebirth. The New Beginning. The opportunity for Change and change that takes us where we need to go; it's all in the Being.

As I began this book almost a year ago, I confessed I didn't know why and I certainly questioned why I was so emphatically drawn to write a book of this nature. I just followed my Inner Voice. I see now, having followed that voice that directed me, without defining the destination, it was necessary for me to take the first baby step and sit down and begin writing, not knowing that the timing could not be more perfect. Each of us has a calling and the purity of that calling can only come from the Voice within.

Go within, without regard to knowing how or why. Now, more than ever, we need to listen and trust what we know to be true. Don't get lost in the negativity of the times. Find joy and peace and promise by turning inward and connecting with that spirit we call God—the Universal Energy, the Natural Knowing, the Inner Voice, the Spirit Within—whatever it means to you and looks like in your eyes.

It matters not what you call it or where you find it; the time has come that we turn to ourselves inward for the guidance and direction during these challenging times. Search not out there. Search within. Believe not in what will happen for you "out" there, believe completely and totally of what will happen for you "in" there, inside yourself. You are a brilliant child of God. The Universal Energy will reward you with abundance when you grab onto the rope tow of life. Begin now. The power in your life is YOU.

A PRACTICE OF BEING

Do we have a choice when we come into this life
or are we pre-destined?
Is our journey to struggle to get a grip on the voice within?
To tackle the power of the mind and spirit as one.
Aligning our will with the will of a higher spirit or power.
Does enlightenment come to those that find the secret?
The secret of perfect alignment.
Being in the right place at the right time with the right purpose in mind.
Is life about jockeying ourselves
to put ourselves in the right place and time
to find that connectedness?

January 26, 2002
From The Author's Journal
Personal Insights from a Meditation

INDEX

A

Abundance 152
Acceptance 105, 104, 113, 143,
    146, 150, 151, 152, 168
Attachment 119, 120, 124
Attraction, Law of 15, 21, 29
Awakening 3, 2, 17, 105, 116,
    177

B

Balance 29, 33, 38
Be Still 36, 33

C

Courage 77, 78, 82, 140, 149

D

Defense mechanisms 42
Detours, see also Setbacks 109,
    110, 113, 115, 116, 117
Dreams 135

F

Faith 77, 78, 82, 106, 107, 140
Fear 95, 116, 149, 153, 162

G

God 1, 5, 18, 19, 20, 22, 28, 29,
    30, 44, 46, 50, 53, 56, 65,
    70, 71, 72, 73, 72, 133,
    134, 136, 137, 152, 153,
    159, 163, 164, 170, 171,
    177, 180
Gratitude 136, 153, 171
Guarantees 103, 105, 150

Guidance 64, 65, 59, 96, 100,
    107, 116, 127, 130, 134,
    135, 140, 149, 151, 155,
    161, 171, 175, 176, 180

H

Hidden Agenda 21

I

Inner Voice 1, 2, 3, 5, 6, 7, 8, 16,
    17, 20, 21, 22, 23, 24, 28,
    29, 43, 45, 51, 59, 63, 60,
    67, 69, 72, 73, 74, 77, 78,
    80, 81, 82, 85, 86, 88, 89,
    90, 91, 95, 96, 97, 98, 99,
    100, 101, 103, 104, 105,
    106, 107, 115, 116, 119,
    125, 127, 128, 129, 133,
    134, 135, 136, 139, 140,
    141, 142, 144, 145, 146,
    149, 150, 151, 152, 153,
    154, 156, 159, 162, 163,
    164, 167, 168, 169, 170,
    171, 172, 175, 176, 177,
    179
Inspiration 28, 68, 156
Intuition 1, 8, 5, 28, 49, 135

J

Journal, author's 24, 31, 65, 74,
    83, 92, 96, 98, 101, 107,
    117, 125, 131, 137, 146,
    156, 159, 165, 172, 180

K

Karma 29, 105, 161, 177

L

Listen 6, 8, 21, 37, 41, 85, 86,
        103, 104, 127, 128, 129,
        131, 139, 142, 155, 162,
        164, 171, 170

M

Meditation 1, 4, 19, 31, 37, 39,
        43, 44, 46, 53, 54, 56, 65,
        74, 83, 87, 92, 96, 180,
        100, 106, 117, 125, 127,
        130, 131, 134, 137, 159,
        163, 164, 165, 171
Myth (we have to be special) 3,
        163, 168, 169, 171

O

Opportunity 109, 140, 146, 152,
        176
Outcome 109, 119, 120, 124,
        142, 143, 145, 150

P

Perceptions 42
Perseverence 78
Personal Insights 25, 26, 32, 40,
        47, 48, 57, 58, 66, 74, 93,
        107, 108, 118, 126, 132,
        138, 147, 158, 166, 173
Perspective 149, 151
Practicality 103
Practice of Being 23, 31, 39, 46,
        55, 64, 74, 82, 91, 100,
        107, 117, 124, 131, 146,
        164, 171

Q

Quiet time 38, 39, 170

R

Resistance 115, 116, 160
Routine 127, 128, 134

S

Setbacks 70, 104, 107, 109, 110,
        114
Source 19, 43, 97, 125, 177
Spiritual Intelligence 16, 17, 98
Stream of consciousness 96
Surrender 22, 63, 70, 143, 145,
        146, 155, 162, 171, 177
Synergy 73, 128, 130

T

Truth 15

U

Understanding 72, 95, 99, 100,
        101, 103, 107, 116, 142,
        170, 176
Universal Energy 5, 16, 17, 18,
        27, 28, 29, 30, 111, 129,
        130, 131, 135, 136, 137,
        140, 141, 143, 152, 177,
        180

W

Willingness 139

ABOUT THE AUTHOR

Mark Hughes began his journey as an advocate for family education when he discovered with his first-born child there were more classes available for dog obedience than parenting. In 1994, he founded the Satori Institute and became certified as a Family Wellness Instructor. He introduced family education for the entire family by offering week-long retreats at youth camps that boasted "a lot of fun and a little education, too."

Loma Smith Photography

In 2002, Mark became a speaker and facilitator for a Southern California based seminar company, *Productive Learning & Leisure* and enjoyed a prosperous experience coaching parents and young adults to be their very best. With a natural talent for inspiring youth and awakening parents, Mark went on to obtain certification as a facilitator for the 'Redirecting Children's Behavior' program offered by *The International Network of Children and Families*. In an effort to make family education available to everyone, and in honor of his 84-year-old mother, Karma, Mark formed a non-profit organization, *The Karma Institute*, a project of the Congressional District Programs. In 2007, Mark developed and facilitated a workshop designed for both parents and teens, 'The Parent and the Teen: Preparing Yourself for Independence.' His expertise in "bridging the gap" prompted Mark to offer his services to business owners as an employee benefit with his Family Crisis Coaching and assist companies and colleges with understanding the Millennial Generation.

I Am Not a Prophet, Therefore I Know, having lain dormant for almost twenty years, was inspired by his personal spiritual awakening and his desire to share how very ordinary people can live their authentic journey by listening to the Inner Voice. Mark has a daughter at San Diego State and a son at Wilsonville High School and balances his time between Portland and Southern California.

PRESENTATIONS & WORKSHOPS

Mr. Hughes delivers powerful and insightful presentations and workshops to audiences around the globe. His intuition and ability to tap into his divine guidance promises a spontaneous and interactive seminar or keynote speech.

In addition to presentations and workshops based on this book, *"Dispelling the Myth We Have to Be Special to Hear The Inner Voice,"* Mark is available to speak to churches, colleges, universities or other social and business organizations on the following topics:

"Disappointments and Disasters: Overcoming Adversity"

How we choose to respond to disappointments and disasters makes all the difference in the world. Change is simply a detour that offers a new way of looking at things. These detours are intended to open our eyes and demonstrate to us how we may have been off-track and provide an opportunity for us to re-align our talents and skills with a new direction in life.

"Family Crisis Coaching at Work"

It is estimated that about 24% of unexcused absenteeism is attributed to issues in the home. Decrease the conflicts at home, and you will find a more productive employee at work. Mark offers several workshops for employers to help their employees have healthier lifestyles in the home and thereby increase productivity at work.

●──────────●

"Mark Hughes is a consummate professional and his presentation style can best be described as engaging, warm and sincere."

Mark LeBlanc
2007-2008 President, National Speakers' Association

"Recruiting, Training, and Retaining Millennials"

Business owners must learn new skills when recruiting and training the Millennial Generation. Mark's material shares ways to create an environment that attracts and retains this new employee and also offers education to parents that empowers their children to learn invaluable life skills so they are better prepared to cope with the challenges that come in today's work place.

"The Parent and the Teen: Preparing Yourself for Independence"

This interactive workshop introduces simple but powerful principles that prepare children to be self-sufficient and take responsibility for the decisions they make. It also teaches the parent how to create a safe environment for honest, respectful communication that results in mutual respect of both the parent and the child.

"Building a Life Plan for the Entire Family"

This workshop is designed for the entire family. It outlines and emphasizes the importance of everyone's participation and contribution to the family both individually and collectively. Each family member accepts responsibility for a collaborative Family Life Plan with clearly defined family goals.

"Changing Roles: The Breadwinner and the Breadmaker"

With divorce, families are forced to make adjustments that they are not prepared for. For the father, it may now be time to assume new responsibilities in the home and connect with his children in new and different ways. Altogether different, the mother is now forced to balance a new job with her duties at home. Learn simple steps to get your world back on track, learning first to take care of yourself, and secondly, how to be the best single parent you can be.

"Living Karma: Doing What is Right"

This insightful look at how Karma will change your life will leave you with a resolve to respond to your life in a whole new way. It is time for a new era of listening, redirecting, and always doing what is the right thing to do.

"Mark has such a natural way of drawing in his audience—because he cares. His enthusiasm and knowledge about his topic translates into an educational and effective presentation that you don't want to miss."

Jennifer Powers
President, National Speakers Association, Oregon Chapter

●————————————————●

For more details about presentations and workshops offered by Mr. Hughes, plus information about quantity discounts of this book, visit our website at:

www.KarmaInstitute.org

or contact the publisher at:
KARMA PUBLISHING
PO Box 3554
Wilsonville, Oregon 97070-3554
(503) 819-3642

Additional copies of this book are available through bookstores, or by mail from the publisher.